Divorce: The Art of Screwing Up Your Children

Divorce: The Art of Screwing Up Your Children

Howard Drutman, Ph.D.

TAOSU

Copyright © 2016 Howard Drutman

All rights reserved.

No part of this publication may be reproduced, stored in a retrieval system, or transmitted, in any form or by any means, without the prior permission in writing of the publisher, nor be otherwise circulated in any form of binding or cover other than that in which it is published and without a similar condition including this condition being imposed on the subsequent purchaser.

For quantity discounts or permission to reproduce part of this book, contact:

Howard Drutman, Ph.D.
900 Old Roswell Lakes Parkway, Suite 340
Roswell, GA 30076

Email Dr. Drutman from his websites:
www.AtlantaBehavioralConsultants.com
www.TheArtOfScrewingUp.com

The Prince of Tides movie quote, Copyright 1991, used by permission of the Producer: Barbra Streisand

Published by TAOSU

ISBN: 978-1-5002-4316-6

Library of Congress Cataloging-in-Publication Data:

Drutman, Howard
Divorce: The Art of Screwing Up Your Children

First Edition

Library of Congress Control Number: 2014911185

DISCLAIMER

The first portion of each section of this book are works of satire, parody, and humor meant solely for entertainment purposes. The recommendations in those portions of the book are a parody and not meant to be followed. Following any advice in those portions of the book could be damaging to you and your children. The author, publisher, and anyone associated with this book will not be liable to any reader for any damages including direct, indirect, incidental, special, consequential, or punitive damages arising out of or in connection with the use of the information contained in this book.

The second portion of each section of this book is designed to provide accurate and authoritative information about the subject matters covered. It is sold with the understanding that the publisher and the author are not engaged in rendering legal, mental health, or other professional services. The information in this book is not intended to replace the services of a qualified mental health professional or attorney.

Identifying information of individuals has been changed to preserve anonymity.

Typesetting services by BOOKOW.COM

To the many forensic clients who have shared their stories with me, thank you. You taught me, with your outrageous ideas and behavior, that you had mastered the art of screwing up your children with your divorce. You were the inspiration for this book.

Acknowledgments

To Judy, my wife and best friend. Your feedback on this book, at times painful, was critically important to the overall presentation of the ideas. I am grateful for your daily support and for allowing me to indulge in the writing of this book.

To Nicole Warshak, my editor: You took my drafts and made critical changes that turned my document into a real book. You are an amazing editor. Thank you. I hope others will use your editorial skills. (NWarshak@gmail.com)

To my cartoon artist, Gwendy Gale Delos Santos, thank you for your humorus cartoon interpretations of the concepts in this book. (gwendy85.deviantart.com)

Thank you to my office colleagues and best friends, Marsha Schechtman, LCSW and Nancy Rosenblum, LCSW for your care, concern, friendship and assistance with this book.

Thank you to my draft readers: Sarah Bakhshi, Psy.D., Autumn Conley, Jamie Drutman, Rita Hollingsworth, James E. Holmes, Esq. (of counsel, Shewmaker & Shewmaker), David Martindale, Ph.D., Julie Morelli, Kevin Richards, Ph.D., Richard Warshak, Ph.D., Mike Wade, Melissa Wilson, and the Hon. Cynthia D. Wright, for providing critical feedback on various drafts of this book.

Lastly, I would like to thank my children, Allison, Benjamin, and

Jamie for loving me, even though I unfortunately practiced some of the concepts in this book. You have taught me much, I love each of you and am so proud of all of you.

Howard Drutman
Roswell, Georgia
April, 2016

"I don't know when my parents began their war against each other - but I do know the only prisoners they took were their children."

Tom Wingo in The Prince of Tides (Movie)

Contents

Introduction	1
Chapter One: The Basics Of Screwing Up Your Children	3
Escalate The Conflict At Every Opportunity	3
Always Win, Don't Give In	6
Don't Break The News Gently	8
Blame Your Spouse	11
Blame The Children	13
Spread The Word Around Town	16
Chapter Two: Screwing Up Your Kids While Divorcing	19
Hire A Shark	19
Divorce: Many Types, Only One For You	22
Monopolize Custody, Visitation, And Parenting Time	27
Take Every Penny And Make It Work For You	31
Dictate All Major Decisions	34
Let It All Hang Out In The Courtroom	38
Time To Get Some Assistance	40
Manipulate The Shrink	43
Exploit Your Spouse's Mental Illness	46
Con The Child Custody Evaluator	49
Lean On Your Children	54
Chapter Three: Screwing Up Co-Parenting	58
Make Your Child Your Messenger	58
Conduct Interrogations	61
Create Uneasy Transitions	63

Be Selfish 67
Mess With Phone Calls, Video Chats, Texts, And Emails 69
Ruin Holidays And Summer Vacations 73
Have Different Rules At Each Home 76
Don't Be Flexible 79
Point Out Your Ex's Parenting Mistakes 81
Relocate 84
Abandon Your Children 87
Sabotage Co-Parenting Counseling 90
Screw Up Your Children's Milestones 94
Dive Into A New Relationship 98
Batter Your Ex's Boyfriend 102
Start A Family Feud 103
Litigate Over And Over Again 105
Alienate The Other Parent 108
Rewrite History 112

Chapter Four: Screwing up the Everyday   **116**
Remarry A Monster 116
Air Your Grievances Online 119
Dress For Success 122
Don't Worry About Child Development 124
Drown Your Sorrows 127
Proclaim Your Moral Superiority 129
Protect Your Kids From All Of The World's Dangers . 133
Ruin Your Children's Activities 137
Preschoolers Need Cell Phones 139
Administer The Silent Treatment 141
Exploit Family Time 143
Never Apologize 145
Get Creative 147

Final Thoughts: Getting Serious For A Moment   **150**
Afterward 150

About The Author   **153**

Introduction

Many years ago I read a book titled *Drawing on the Right Side of the Brain* by Betty Edwards. One innovative technique in the book directs budding artists to focus not on the object they are drawing, but on the negative space that borders the object. This uncommon approach helps many improve their ability to draw. By looking at the object from a different perspective, the artist can better grasp its shape and design and more easily transmit it to paper.

I have approached this book using a similar technique. By recommending, sarcastically, the wrong way to parent, I hope you will see more clearly how to raise happy, confident children. As you see how parents screw up their children, you will simultaneously be learning what behaviors to avoid before, during, and after your divorce. This book's concept is pretty simple. Do you want to screw up your children? Then follow the insincere advice in this book. But, if you want to parent successfully, avoid the things I show will harm your children. And if you see yourself in the book's recommendations, stop and change course. Your children will certainly thank you for it.

This book is written for people who are contemplating divorce, divorcing, or living in the wake of a divorce. The ideas come from my experiences helping hundreds of parents who have been through these transitions. Parenting is difficult in general, but parenting through divorce can be overwhelming. This book provides the guidance you need in a form that offers some comic relief.

NOTE ON THE USE OF PRONOUNS: Within each chapter, examples refer to husbands and wives or daughters and sons. While various familial titles and gender-specific pronouns are used ("him," "her," "their father," "their mother," "the ex," or "your spouse"), they apply to all, including same-sex couples. After all, why should heterosexual couples be the only ones allowed to screw up their children?

Chapter One: The Basics Of Screwing Up Your Children

Escalate The Conflict At Every Opportunity

You're getting divorced. Years of conflict have taken their toll. Now is the time to accelerate the conflict so you can power through your divorce and come out on top. And, if you do it right, you will royally screw up your kids in the process.

Conflict got you into this situation. Now, you must use your skills in every encounter with your spouse to ensure that you get everything, leaving your spouse humiliated, defeated, and broke. Pay no mind to the fact that your children will be caught in the crossfire. When you win one fight, go right on to the next. Keep the battle alive!

Be sure that your children are fully aware of the hostility between you and their other parent. Be expressive. Be antagonistic. Be loud. Be physical. Putting your fist through a wall is genius.

Conflict is the struggle for power. Once you have the power you can establish control. Once you have control, you can shut your spouse out of your life and the lives of your children. Make it your goal to walk away from every interaction with your spouse knowing that you have come out victorious, even if winning the battle means losing the war.

Embarrass your children with angry rants in front of their friends. Yell and scream just like some of those reality TV stars. Scream loud enough for your neighbors to hear. This will clearly demonstrate to your kids that controlling your emotions in public is simply unnecessary.

Parental conflict is toxic when spouses are unable to resolve their differences in a civilized, respectful manner. It includes yelling, blaming and name-calling and can escalate to intimidation — in extreme cases, violence. This incessant behavior creates a volatile environment filled with tension, hostility, fear, and contempt.

Children need predictability and stability, and child development experts agree that chronic parental conflict exacts a toll. The ensuing chaos and tension makes children feel vulnerable, scared, and insecure and can leave them anxious and depressed. They may also begin to exhibit behavioral problems such as fighting with peers, poor school performance, and even drug or alcohol abuse.

Chapter One: The Basics Of Screwing Up Your Children

Your angry tirades in public humiliate your children. They feel embarrassed knowing others are judging you, and their self-esteem suffers as a result. Whether in public or private, your children internalize your criticism of your spouse. They will be ashamed of the personality traits, looks, and mannerisms they have inherited that remind you of their other parent. They fear that you will reject them as well.

You are a role model for your children, and when you model high conflict, they believe it is an appropriate, acceptable way to resolve disagreements. They will grow up to terrorize and disrespect others, including their own parents. They will engage in similar fights with their future partners and damage those relationships. Also, since your behavior will negatively impact your children's romantic relationships, you will also hurt your children's children. Quite a family legacy you will leave for generations to come.

- How To Screw Up Your Children -

- Maintain high levels of conflict with your spouse/ex-spouse.

(Your children will feel vulnerable, scared, and insecure.)

- Pressure your children to take your side in any argument with their other parent.

(Your children will feel that if they side with you, they will anger their other parent. If they side with their other parent, you will be furious. If they stay neutral, both of their parents will be disappointed with them.)

- Scream and use disrespectful, demeaning language toward your spouse in front of your children.

(Your children will believe it is okay to terrorize others and speak disrespectfully to others.)

Always Win, Don't Give In

"Winning isn't everything. It's the only thing." Vince Lombardi was right.

In the game of divorce, the stakes are high, and the competition is intense. You are playing to win. Every argument. Every interaction. Every point.

You could perfect your strategy by studying some of the great champions of our time. Lance Armstrong beat cancer and went on to win the Tour de France seven consecutive times. How? Years of training, hard work, and the desire to win at all cost. Former San Francisco Giant Barry Bonds is recognized as one of the greatest baseball players of all time. He holds the record for most career home runs hit. Why? He gave everything he had to crush the competition. And if Tom Brady threw even one bad pass it could have ruined his chances at another Super Bowl ring. Each of these champions was not afraid to think outside the box and use extreme tactics, even illegal or questionable ones, to insure victory. Every move counts, because everything is on the line. Got the point? Good.

Remember, it's never WHAT is right, but WHO is right that matters. You are going to want to be right 100% of the time. This means never giving up, never giving in, and never (NEVER!) accepting defeat.

To clinch the win, you can not just play aggressive offense, you must also play brilliant defense. It is not enough to be right; your spouse must be wrong. Twist his or her arguments around, especially the ones that are not entirely flawed. Make it clear that you are a winner, and that he or she is a loser. Don't hesitate to convey your negative opinion of your spouse to your children. They must know the truth about their other parent.

CHAPTER ONE: THE BASICS OF SCREWING UP YOUR CHILDREN

When you insist on always being right, you are hurting your children. They likely see you as a know-it-all and a bully, and they are learning your cruel and destructive interaction style that will likely damage their future romantic relationships. Your children feel deflated watching you demoralize their other parent, and when they see you treat your spouse with hostility and disrespect, they will become angry with you for perpetuating the conflict.

Forget winning. Live your life by another clichéd sports saying instead: "It's not whether you win or lose, but how you play the game that matters." Your children will thank you for it.

- How To Screw Up Your Children -

- **Adopt the attitude, "It's not what's right, but who's right that matters."**

(Your children will learn that it is more important to win arguments than it is to act with honor.)

- **Demean your ex in front of your children.**

(Your children will believe it is acceptable to treat others with contempt, including their future spouses. They will also resent you for mistreating their other parent.)

- Never admit you are wrong.

(You will teach your children to be inflexible and unwilling to admit to any mistakes or errors.)

Don't Break The News Gently

When you break the news to your children that you are getting divorced, do not spare their feelings. Do not, as the experts suggest, assure them that the divorce is not their fault, that both their parents love them, and that their lives will remain calm and stable. You do this your way.

Schedule this discussion with your children when your spouse is out of town or preoccupied with a work deadline. If you blindside your spouse, you can control the conversation. There is no chance your children will believe this divorce is a mutual decision if you present the news without your spouse present. Let your children know that the divorce is not your fault; you are the one fighting to keep the family together. Now is the time to place the blame on someone else.

Let your children know you love them. At the same time, let them know your love is much deeper than their other parent's love. It must be. You are the one that brushed your daughter's hair, planned your children's birthday parties, and went trick-or-treating on Halloween. I mean you are the one spending the time to carry on this discussion with them, aren't you?

Let your children know their lives will be taking a radical turn, and that you have no idea where they will end up. Tell them you don't know where they'll be living or with whom they will be living. It's up to the courts to decide custody. It could be in a house,

CHAPTER ONE: THE BASICS OF SCREWING UP YOUR CHILDREN

an apartment, or under a freeway overpass for all you know. They might have to pick up and move to California, North Dakota, or Berlin, Germany. Warn them money might get a little tight, and you might have to make cutbacks on piano lessons, tutors, or summer camp. Nothing is certain at this point.

The prevailing opinion among mental health professionals is that parents should inform their children of their divorce together. This presents a united front and prevents the children from feeling they must take sides. Parents must assure their children the divorce is not their fault, and refrain from placing blame on each other. If you hold your spouse accountable for the divorce, your children will have

a polarized view of their parents, seeing you as good and their other parent as bad, which is not healthy for them.

When you tell your children you are divorcing, you must also let them know that most things will remain constant. Children crave stability and predictability, and if you share the potential uncertainty of the future, you will increase their worry and anxiety. They are already stressed about the reorganization of their family, and additional worry will further jeopardize your children's mental health. Of course, the breakup of their family prevents things from returning to the way things were before the divorce, but you must reassure your children that eventually things will settle down, and their lives will go back to a new normal.

- How To Screw Up Your Children -

- Tell your children about the divorce without your spouse present.

(This may confuse your children and leave them feeling unsure of what is really going on.)

- Let the children know that you love them more than their other parent.

(Your children will be conflicted between what you have told them and the actions of their other parent. Also, children want to be loved by both of their parents.)

- Tell your children that life will radically change, and you are uncertain of how things will end up.

(Your children will be filled with anxiety and fear over the future.)

CHAPTER ONE: THE BASICS OF SCREWING UP YOUR CHILDREN

Blame Your Spouse

If you are the one who left the marriage, tell your children that you were driven away. If you are the husband, tell your children their mother is cold and withholding and can't even make decent lasagna. She was never a good wife and always takes you for granted. Blame her for your affair. After all, if you had a good partner, you never would have strayed, and the family would still be together. The divorce is not your fault.

Let your children know how much happier you will be divorced. Tell them how stifling married life is and how thrilling and fulfilling your life will be. Your talents can finally be displayed for the world to see. You can now focus on achieving fame and fortune. Nothing will hold you back from reaching your potential.

If your spouse left you, it's even easier to place blame. Tell your children their father betrayed them by having an affair. He was never cut out to be a dad and simply does not love the family enough to fight for the marriage. It is all his fault. You should have a field day milking the sadness, grief, and loss. The emotional pain you are experiencing gives you a pass when it comes to routine life tasks. How can you get a job when you are so distraught? How can you possibly keep your mind on work when your life is falling apart?

Let your children know how bad you feel. Gain their sympathy at every opportunity, and use this as an excuse to pull back from active parenting. You have taken care of them; now it's their turn to take care of you.

* * *

Divorce: The Art of Screwing Up Your Children

Mental health professionals strongly urge parents not to share their spouse's misdeeds with their children. Children are not mature enough to comprehend fully that even when it seems one spouse is at fault, usually the marriage had weaknesses to which both spouses contributed. Initially, the children may listen to your complaints and allegations about their other parent. However, eventually, the children will either lose respect for that parent or redirect their anger at you for your badmouthing. Either way, the children are left with feelings of anger for one or both of their parents.

If you hold your spouse solely accountable for your divorce, your children will learn it is okay to blame others for their troubles. They may come to believe that they are not the ones that are in control of their lives. Sharing the responsibility for your divorce, on the other hand, teaches your children they must take responsibility for their behaviors and control their destiny.

Chapter One: The Basics Of Screwing Up Your Children

- How To Screw Up Your Children -

- Blame the divorce on your spouse.

(Your children will learn to blame their partners rather than take responsibility for problems in their relationships.)

- Tell your children the marriage has held you back from leading a fulfilling life.

(Your children will feel they too are the cause of your unhappiness.)

- Constantly remind your children how devastated you are about the divorce.

(This disclosure will burden your children and make them feel responsible for taking care of you.)

Blame The Children

Maybe the fault does not lie with you or your spouse. After all, it was the stress of raising your children that led to the breakdown of your marriage. Those little monsters cost you a fortune, and you and your spouse fought over everything from discipline and education to nutrition and bedtime. The financial and emotional drain on your resources left you depleted and unable to handle the stress of family life. Obviously, it was their fault, and you should let them know it.

Let your children know what your life would look like if you didn't have the obligation of caring for them. You would have more time to devote to your career and more money to spend on yourself. You would be a successful artist or the CEO of a Fortune 500 company. If it weren't for them, you would be very famous and widely respected like Bill Gates. At the very least, you would be traveling the world in style. Tell the kids that now that you will have time without them, you will finally have the freedom to pursue your passions.

Get specific with your children. It is not just the act of raising any child that has made married life so intolerable. It is your children, specifically, that carry many of the same character traits you dislike so much in your spouse. Say things like, "You are stubborn, just like your mother." Identify and be critical of the character flaws your children inherited from their other parent.

Telling your children that they are responsible for the breakdown of your marriage transfers the culpability off of you and your spouse and onto your children. The reality is your children did not cause your relationship problems. Being stressed by your parental responsibilities is your issue to manage, not your children's. As it is, children have a

Chapter One: The Basics Of Screwing Up Your Children

tendency to blame themselves for their parents' divorce. If you blame them, your children will be left feeling completely responsible, and they may very well carry this guilt for the rest of their lives. It is, therefore, imperative to make sure your children understand that they had nothing to do with the breakdown of the marriage.

It is also important that you never accuse your children of impeding your success. Your children will experience guilt, worry, and misplaced responsibility if they believe they have held you back from finding happiness. Ultimately, they will feel bad about themselves for being a burden to you.

Your children realize there are things you despise about your ex, but pointing out these traits in your children makes them feel ashamed. They learn to dislike these parts of themselves and may believe that, because they share these characteristics with your ex, you dislike them too. Eventually, this can spiral into self-hatred.

- How To Screw Up Your Children -

- Blame your children for the divorce.

(They will feel responsible for the breakdown of the family, and will be consumed with guilt, sadness and self-hatred for the rest of their lives.)

- Tell your children they have held you back from reaching your potential.

(Your children will feel they are a burden to you. They will also learn to feel responsible for other people's behavior.)

- Let your children know you dislike things about them that are like their other parent.

(Your children will begin to despise those parts of their character, and it will destroy their self-esteem.)

Spread The Word Around Town

Change your Facebook status to *single* and post the update "I do. I did. Now I'm done." Rock a t-shirt with the phrase *"Under New Management."* It's time to let everyone know you are getting divorced.

If you have been wronged, hit hard with a well-crafted public relations campaign. Pile your ex's clothes on the curb outside the house, and let the neighbors know how terrible things have gotten between you two. Spread the word organically by badmouthing your ex to every friend, family member, parent, teacher, pediatrician, dentist, postman, dance instructor, and baseball coach. The more you talk, the faster the information will disseminate. To be certain you've covered your bases, take out a billboard announcing to the world that he's a cheat and a liar, and pay for it with your joint bank account.

Maybe you are just plain happy to be done with your marriage. If so, you'll want everyone to know you are better off on your own. "AHH FREE" makes a great vanity plate! Cruise around town and spread the word that you are single and ready to mingle.

Throw yourself a divorce party. Make it as cool as those divorce celebrations that *The Real Housewives* have on TV. Invite your friends and family to celebrate your renewed independence with some martinis and mini hot dogs. Post pictures of your party on social media, and remember, there is no such thing as bad publicity.

***

CHAPTER ONE: THE BASICS OF SCREWING UP YOUR CHILDREN

Your children are horrified when other people know the intimate details of their lives. This embarrassment is particularly true for adolescents, as they hate it when other people know their personal business. The humiliation will likely spiral into shame, and they will be haunted by it throughout their adult lives.

Badmouthing your ex around town will create a disaster. It will be so uncomfortable for your children to be around their other parent they will start to avoid him or her completely. Also, they may start to avoid you since you are the source of the information. Either way, your children's relationship with one or both of their parents will deteriorate.

The truth is no one wants to know all the details of your marriage and divorce. Keep your private failings private, keep your ex's indiscretions to yourself and don't make this cause for celebration. Your children will ultimately thank you for letting your divorce slip under the radar.

* * *

- How To Screw Up Your Children -

- Let everyone know that you are getting divorced.

(Your children will be embarrassed that their parents' conflict has been made public.)

- Let everyone know your ex has wronged you.

(Your children will feel uncomfortable when they are with him or her in public. They will be angry with you for badmouthing their other parent and creating this situation.)

- Celebrate your divorce.

(You are insensitive to the fact that this is a very difficult time for your children.)

Chapter Two: Screwing Up Your Kids While Divorcing

Hire A Shark

Hiring the right divorce attorney is critical. It can mean the difference between a life lived happily ever after or a starring role in your very own Greek tragedy. For this reason, you must consider your options carefully.

Hire an attorney who is up for the fight of his or her life. If the attorney even mentions mediation or collaborative divorce, run for the hills. That lawyer is interested in mitigating the conflict, putting the matter to rest quickly, and letting you move on with your life. These kinds of attorneys will certainly try to talk you into negotiating a settlement and are willing to let your ex off the hook without taking responsibility for destroying your marriage and ruining your life. This does not work for you. Your goal is to make your ex regret the day he or she met you.

You need a shark. A shark is laser focused on obtaining the greatest financial and custodial settlement possible. This means fighting on no matter how much pain and suffering it causes you and your family. Trivial matters like the best interest of the children will not sidetrack a shark, and he or she does not buy into the psychobabble of a custody evaluator or the silly opinions of a court-appointed guardian. This attorney will not allow for negotiation strategies that require you to compromise anything. A shark will fight, fight, fight! These sharks will not stop until your ex-husband concedes, the judge finds in your favor, or you are completely bankrupt.

Sharks cost a lot of money, of course. That is precisely how you can weed out the weaklings. If the attorney does not require a retainer commensurate with your children's college tuition, he or she does not make the cut. His suits should be custom tailored or designed by Mr. Armani himself. Her dresses must be hot off the latest runways of Paris. The attorney's office should brandish Ivy League diplomas, expensive antiques, and a view of the city that will take your breath away. Obviously, the higher up the office is in a high-rise building, the better the attorney. Just think of how intimidated your ex and his sorry-excuse-for-a-lawyer will be when they come to your attorney's office for a settlement negotiation meeting. Revenge is so sweet.

One last thing, before you settle on your attorney, be sure to have an initial consultation with lawyers from every prominent family law firm in your area. This clever strategy will disqualify those firms from representing your spouse. The cost for the consultation is nothing compared to the payoff you'll receive by blocking your spouse from hiring any of the top attorneys in your city.

***

CHAPTER TWO: SCREWING UP YOUR KIDS WHILE DIVORCING

Sharks may take advantage of you for their financial gain. The longer the litigation drags out, the more money they make. For these reasons, they do not want to settle the case until they win or you run out of money. This strategy will prolong your children's exposure to parental conflict and hostility, thereby, adding stress to your children's lives. Sharks often do not put the best interest of the children first, and might even ignore the recommendations of forensic mental health professionals, child custody evaluators, and guardians or discredit the professionals if it serves them well. The cost of hiring this type of attorney may leave you destitute after the case is concluded. Then you may find yourself in a position where you can not afford to meet the basic needs of your children.

- How To Screw Up Your Children -

- Hire a shark.

(This attorney looks out for your interests, but not necessarily the best interest of your children.)

- Spend tons of money to hire an expensive lawyer.

(This will leave you with less money to care for your children.)

- Do not settle. Take the case all the way to trial.

(This will prolong the divorce and expose your children to high levels of parental conflict over a long period.)

Divorce: Many Types, Only One For You

There are many ways to divorce. Some methods involve more conflict than others. Do not choose the easy way out. Seize the opportunity to inflict maximum emotional and financial pain on your ex and, ultimately, screw up your children as best you can.

Some people choose to file uncontested or no-fault divorces. This is not for you. No-fault divorces imply that you and your ex are equally responsible, and you want everyone to know it is your spouse's fault that the marriage ended. You don't want to give the impression that you and your spouse are working together for the best interest of the children. If you got along that well, wouldn't you still be married? Since a no-fault divorce is out of the question, you must be very careful in selecting the right type of divorce process.

Mediation (No way!)

Mediation is an alternative form of dispute resolution that utilizes a neutral third party rather than a judge. Essentially, it is a way for the courts to save money and for lazy judges to take on fewer cases. Do not fall for this scam. If you mediate your divorce and come to an agreement, your settlement is complete and just awaits the judge's signature. Just like that, the conflict is over. A settlement means that your children's lives will be less stressful, and if you want to screw them up, this certainly will not help. Mediation also utilizes a process called caucusing, where the divorcing parties are placed in separate rooms, and the mediator goes back and forth with proposals until an agreement is reached. This takes all of the joy out of seeing your ex cringe with embarrassment when you spell out the details of her cosmetic surgeries or his erectile dysfunction. Under no circumstances should you settle your case in mediation. You deserve your day in court.

Arbitration (Not a chance!)

With arbitration, you and your spouse agree on an attorney or retired judge to preside over a trial and render a decision. This approach is an equally terrible idea. A private trial with an arbitrator is likely to be confidential, and all that dirt you want to dish on your ex may never end up on public record. Also, arbitrators are likely to hear the case quickly, denying you the lengthy wait for a traditional court date and less time to inflict strain on your spouse and your kids.

Collaborative Divorce (Never!)

A third approach is the collaborative divorce. This process involves a team of attorneys, mental health coaches, a financial professional, and child specialist that work with you and your spouse to settle your divorce. If you fail to settle, the collaborative process requires that the team withdraws, and the parties hire new attorneys and try again. Your goal is to keep the conflict going on as long as possible by refusing to settle, so this process is also unacceptable. The collaborative divorce specialists also insist that you act respectfully throughout the process. You are not looking to be respectful; you are out for blood.

Litigation (Yes! Yes! Yes!)

Litigation is the only viable option. You will bring your action before the court and let the judge decide the outcome of the case. It allows you to claim injury, find fault, and to punish your ex for your pain, and, therefore, offers more opportunities for conflict than any other method of divorce. You will be free to share your story in a courtroom and put it all on public record. All of your grievances, all of your spouse's shortcomings, and all of his or her transgressions will be documented, and they will be available for your friends, your family, and your children to see. And just an added bonus, you could drag out the litigation by requesting documentation, interrogatories, depositions, hearings, and a trial. This will certainly keep your ex from moving on with his or her life.

Participating in high conflict litigation is also a very easy way to screw up your children. Have them join you in court so you can ride the emotional rollercoaster together. Keep your children updated on the litigation, including all of your court dates, discussions, mediation, and discovery, and be sure to leave the most damaging legal documents in plain sight for them to read. This will provide them with quite an education. Imagine their vast new vocabulary; "affidavit…election…motion…infidelity."

* * *

Chapter Two: Screwing Up Your Kids While Divorcing

Litigation is a time of intense hostility, anger, and gamesmanship. Your children are exposed to high levels of conflict and uncertainty, and the unpredictability of the legal process will likely cause them to feel anxious about their future. Additionally, they feel pressure to side with both of their parents. In your presence, your children will hide their honest feelings for fear of hurting you or getting you angry. They will tell each parent what they think that parent wants to hear just to please them. And because contentious litigations can go on and on, your children remain in the middle of your intense conflict for a long period.

You should do your best to shield your children from the legal process. They do not have the understanding to put complex legal concepts into perspective, and they are likely to mistake the implications of the information that you share. In addition, hearing two very different sides of the story from both of their parents makes it difficult for children to decide which parent to believe, and causes them to doubt both parents. Ultimately, your children lose faith that they can turn to either parent for advice or help to understand the things going on in their life.

Hearing details of their parents' bad behavior and reading documents containing disturbing allegations about their parents is damaging to children. With litigation, the information is public and accessible to everyone. Children should not know about their parents' mental health issues, sexual behavior, or history of legal problems. This is true whether their parents are happily married or in the throws of divorce.

Mediation, arbitration, and collaborative divorce can substantially decrease the stress associated with a divorce. These types of dispute resolution methods discourage conflict between the two parties and are much quicker than waiting for a trial date in court. Also, mediation and arbitration are likely to be confidential. This will shield your children from reading about their parent's misbehaviors and transgressions.

- How To Screw Up Your Children -

- Refuse to participate in mediation, arbitration or collaborative divorce

(This will lead to high conflict litigation.)

- Do not participate in any divorce process other than litigation.

(This will prolong the uncertainty and expose the children to high levels of parental conflict.)

- Leave legal documents that contain disturbing allegations about your spouse lying around so the children can read them.

(This will expose your children to negative information and allegations about one of their parents. Hearing about negative behaviors of a parent leaves children feeling confused and angry.)

CHAPTER TWO: SCREWING UP YOUR KIDS WHILE DIVORCING

Monopolize Custody, Visitation, And Parenting Time

When you go to court, you must fight for sole physical and legal custody of your children. Sole physical custody assures that they will live with you 100% of the time. The meaning of sole legal custody varies in different states and countries, but all that matters is that you will be in control of virtually all aspects of your children's lives. All of the power is in your hands, and effectively, you can exclude your ex both physically and legally. You never have to listen to his input, and you never have to consult him on anything about your children. If you are given joint custody, you will have to split parenting time and you may be required to share decision-making with your ex on important issues. You never ever want to have to share decision-making with your ex. This should be your motivation to do whatever you must to win sole custody. As a bonus, obtaining custody makes it obvious to the world that you are the competent parent and your ex is a total loser.

In order to obtain sole custody, you must argue in court that it would be best to have the children with you seven days a week. They need the stability of living in one home, and that home should be yours. Even if your children are begging for more time with their dad, remember you know best. You found living with your ex to be stressful and at times traumatic. How could it be possible for your children to have a different experience? It has to be stressful for them too. If your legal battle to get sole custody isn't going in your favor, do what you must to turn things around and fabricate outrageous allegations about your ex's fitness as a parent and a person in general.

You feel strongly that your house is your children's one and only home. The message will be clear to them if you dissuade your ex from making his house a happy place for the children to be.

Discourage him from furnishing bedrooms for them; they will not mind sleeping on the pull out couch in his office when they visit. Let the children drag their clothes and toys to their dad's house in heavy suitcases. It is silly to have another closet full of things at a place they are just spending a few nights a month. You want your kids to feel like they are staying the night in a motel, because the more uncomfortable and out of place they feel, the sooner they realize it is not home. Be sure to make your children drag their suitcases to school with them, since their father will be picking them up after school.

If you have to share even a fraction of your parenting time with your ex, do not let anything take away your time with your children. First, put an end to all sleepovers outside of the home. If your children want to spend the night at their friends' places, let them do it during your ex's time, not yours. When your children protest, remind them that your family comes before their friends and to question your rule is selfish. Extracurricular activities will also threaten your time with your children if you are not careful. Try to schedule as many gymnastics classes and music lessons as you can during your ex's parenting time. If he has the children every Wednesday night for dinner, these activities can take place back to back on Wednesday night. Pretty simple. Let him drag them back and forth to these activities. You should, however, make sure to attend the practices or games that coincide with your ex's parenting time every once in a while. You can be the supporting, loving parent while also infuriating him.

Regardless of your parenting schedule, you can always mess with your ex when it comes to transitioning the children to and from your home. Do not let the kids go until the exact time specified in the court order—not a second sooner. If your children are ready, and their father is waiting outside, too bad. You are just obeying the court order. On the other hand, do not push your children to be ready on time for their pickup. If they are getting dressed or playing video games, do not rush them. Your ex can idle in the driveway. Arrive early or late, never on time when you are the one dropping off the children. If you continue to complicate matters, your ex will hate sharing parenting time. Your goal is to push him past his limit so that he requests a modification of the custody agreement and grants you sole physical custody.

When you monopolize custody and restrict your children's access to their other parent, you are not serving their best interest. Your children will miss a strong relationship with their other parent, and it will cause them a lot of heartaches. The mental and emotional benefit your children derive when both parents are involved in their day-to-day lives is extremely important in helping them deal with divorce and life in general.

Your children also suffer when you dictate what they can and can not do during your parenting time. They feel trapped and will become angry with you for having to miss out on time with their friends and the activities they enjoy.

Many non-custodial parents fail to set up their house with the kids clothes, toys, books, etc. Not having personal possessions makes children feel like visitors to someone else's house, not like home. Without personal space and possessions, children feel out of place, unhappy, and anxious to go back to the comforts of home. Also, children find carrying clothes to school in a bag to be a humiliating experience.

- How To Screw Up Your Children -

- Obtain sole legal and physical custody so you can restrict your ex's access to your children.

(Your children will have minimal contact with the other parent, and they will lose the love and support that relationship provides.)

- Forbid your children to participate in activities that take away your parenting time.

(Your children will feel frustrated and trapped.)

- Insist your children transition to their other parent at the exact time ordered by the parenting plan.

(Your children will become aggravated and upset when they are ready to leave your house, but you will not let them leave until the exact time.)

CHAPTER TWO: SCREWING UP YOUR KIDS WHILE DIVORCING

Take Every Penny And Make It Work For You

Every state has procedures and protocols in place to divide marital assets. Some employ community property laws while others follow laws of equitable distribution. Regardless of the process your court uses, there is only one goal: keep as much of the money as you can for yourself and leave your spouse with as little money as possible. Some people say that money is the root of all evil. The only money that is evil is every penny your undeserving spouse gets to keep.

As soon as you know you are divorcing, start hiding your assets. Stockpile cash and purchase a stack of American Express® gift cards that you can use after the settlement is complete. You should also begin moving your valuables into hiding. Stash the crystal from your wedding, your silver serving pieces, and any art that is in storage in your brother's basement or at a friend's hunting lodge. Your spouse will not even realize the stuff is missing. After the divorce, you can sell them on Ebay for extra cash.

Before filing for divorce, check off some things on your "To Do" list. Remember, at this point your spouse is still splitting the tab. Get cosmetic surgery, buy a diamond necklace from Tiffany, and get yourself a Rolex. You will want all of these things once you are on your own, and you will not want to pay for them by yourself.

During your divorce, you will be dividing your homes, cars, furniture, bank accounts, retirement accounts, investments, and other possessions. Take as much as you can. Fight for the family home, the nicer car, and the stock options. The last thing you want is for your ex to maintain a life of luxury while you are living in a motel eating ramen noodles.

At the start of the case, allege that your husband stole money from your joint bank account and stashed it offshore. Do you

31

not have any evidence? No problem. Just making the accusation will taint his character, and he will have to prove his innocence to restore his reputation. That should keep him and his accountants busy for a while, and it will cost him time and money.

If you are seeking child support, take the amount that you were going to propose and add a zero. Child support should not just provide food, clothing, and shelter for the children. It should also cover your new wardrobe, a personal trainer, and your spa vacations. Dream of the lifestyle you want to live and fight for the amount of money you need to make that happen. All you have to do is to pad the budget a bit. If you are not happy with the amount you are awarded, tell the children that their father is cheap, and blame him for everything that you can not afford to buy them.

If you are to receive alimony, tell your husband, the court, and everyone you know that you deserve to live the fabulous lifestyle to which you have become accustomed. "Temporary spousal support" will not work for you; request lifetime alimony payments. You do not need a training period before reentering the workforce because you are never going to work again. You have made many sacrifices for your family. You gave up your career and your happiness for your marriage and your children, and you are entitled to be well taken care of for the rest of your life. If lifetime alimony is out of the question, at least get it to cover the years your children are still living at home.

If you were the breadwinner, and, therefore, the one that will be paying alimony and child support, it is only fair that you constantly remind everyone that you are subsidizing your ex's lifestyle. She just sits on her rear collecting checks. Tell the children that their mother is lazy and incompetent, and she is using their money to fund her social life.

In addition to being critical of your ex, you can also buy your children's love, appreciation, and respect. You should shower your

Chapter Two: Screwing Up Your Kids While Divorcing

children with gifts, making sure they have the latest in fashion and technology and all of the impossible-to-find toys. Naturally, they will like you much better than their mother. Plus, you could use the money, not discipline, to control their behavior. If your ex-wife finds your spending too indulgent, it is only because she is jealous that you have more than her. Don't hesitate to tell her that your money is yours and that you will spend it as you see fit. Let her know she is just mad that she can no longer enjoy the material benefits of your largess.

When you are divorcing, deciding on monetary issues can cause a lot of conflicts. However, there are certain behaviors that you can avoid to lessen the negative effects on your children. Do not hide money or assets. This is against the law, and it teaches your children that it is acceptable to take what is not theirs. Do not falsely allege that your spouse has stolen money or assets or your children will resent you for badmouthing their other parent. Do not complain that your ex is stingy with money or lazy for accepting it from you. This puts your children in the middle of your conflict.

If you end up with the better deal, do not use your money to manipulate your children. Spoiling children with excessive material possessions can hurt their character development. They will grow up feeling entitled, and they will not learn the connection between effort and reward.

- How To Screw Up Your Children -

- Allege that your spouse has stolen marital assets and hidden them.

(Your children will resent your allegation about their other parent.)

- If you pay alimony, constantly remind your children that you are supporting their lazy parent's selfish lifestyle.

(Your children will be angry with you for badmouthing their other parent.)

Dictate All Major Decisions

If the judge grants you joint legal and physical custody, you now have to share your children with your ex. You must not have made her look crazy enough in court. Lucky for you, there is another way to exact control. Ask the judge to grant you "final decision-making" on all issues regarding your children. This will give you the final word on healthcare, education, religion, and extracurricular activities. You must fight for ALL final decision-making, even if you do not care about a particular issue. Remember, it is about power, and you will be the appointed problem solver and the parent in charge.

CHAPTER TWO: SCREWING UP YOUR KIDS WHILE DIVORCING

Even if you have never been to a pediatrician's appointment, fight for medical decision-making. You will now have final decision-making on all of your children's medical, dental, and psychological healthcare issues. It does not matter that you only met the doctor once in the plumbing section of the local hardware store. You have seen every episode of *ER*, and you can look up anything you need to know online. You decide if your children get their tonsils removed and whether or not they wear braces, and you will have the authority to prevent unnecessary and expensive medical treatments such as immunizations and yearly physicals. What is the worst that happens; your child comes down with a preventable disease? These days, there are antibiotics for everything. Furthermore, if you have never really been a fan of modern medicine, you will finally be able to take your kids for the homeopathy, naturopathy, and acupuncture that your ex detests. Having this kind of power will drive her crazy, and you can't buy that type of revenge.

Fight for final decision-making on education as well and you will get to make all decisions regarding academic concerns, including your children's schools, their tutoring, and any special services that are available to them. This power also allows you to switch your children's school whenever you feel like it and as often as you desire. You have the green light to choose a school that is inconvenient to your ex's home or work. This will aggravate both your ex and your children. Two for one! After a while, your children may protest the long drive and ask to stay with you for the entire week.

Whether or not you are religious, it is important to have final decision-making on religious issues. You never know when the Spirit will move you. Now, you will have control over your children's religious education and practice, and if your ex's faith is very important to her, you can really come out ahead. You can keep your children away from her church or get them involved in a religion that contradicts her beliefs. This will make her furious.

Obtaining final decision-making on extracurricular activities means you can control which nights the children participate. Extracurricular activities include all sports, music lessons, art, and dance classes. When choosing, do not consider what might enhance your children's lives; just enroll the children in any activities that take place during their mother's parenting time. She will be stuck taxiing them to and from practices, performances, and games. You will be free to enjoy some relaxation, without taking away from your parenting time.

When you demand decision-making authority in order to keep power and control over your ex, your children suffer. You are shutting out their other parent from providing input into their significant life experiences. Your ex might have helpful insight that could assist in making the best decisions for your children.

If you have ulterior motives, you are likely not making decisions that are in your children's best interest. Specifically, changing schools may cause the children to struggle with new friends, teachers, and activities. Also, feeding your children competing religious theologies will make them anxious and confused as they wrestle over which philosophy is better for them. It will also put them in the middle of their parent's conflict.

Ultimately, your children will realize that you are making decisions just to spite their other parent. When they realize this, they will stop trusting you. They will feel frustrated and angry, but in the long term, they will learn to be spiteful as well, and they will struggle to maintain healthy relationships of their own.

- How To Screw Up Your Children -

- Obtain final decision-making on medical issues, even if you have never been to a doctor's appointment.

(This will result in your children's medical decisions being made by a person who has no experience with their prior healthcare.)

- Use your right of final decision-making on education to switch your children's schools on a regular basis.

(The constant changes will leave your children feeling frustrated and angry. They will also feel sad over the loss of the friends they leave behind.)

- Use all your decision-making authority to exert power and control over your ex-spouse.

(Your children will realize that you are more interested in controlling their other parent than making decisions in their best interest, and they will stop trusting you.)

Let It All Hang Out In The Courtroom

When you appear in court, do not worry about impressing the judge or presenting an image that convinces the court you are a fit parent. Just be you. Your attorneys might even insist you wear a conservative suit and tie to look respectable, but you do not let anyone boss you around. You should do, say, and wear what you want. If they do not like you for whom you are, tough.

If you want to be comfortable and present yourself as a casual person, show up in your weekend attire. Wear sweats and flip flops, and throw on a baseball cap. Keep it casual. This style of dress will signal to the judge that you are stable, relaxed, and Zen-like.

If you want to present a strong, no-nonsense persona, wear a wife-beater shirt bearing the logo of some alcoholic beverage. Jeans, particularly those broken-in ones stained with motorcycle grease and frayed on the knee show you are a man's man, someone who fixes things. Be sure to have your wallet attached to your belt loop by a chain to project an image of safety and security.

If you prefer to use your animal magnetism and allure, wear a low-cut mini-dress, with stilettos and lots of jewelry and make-up. If nothing else, the attorneys and the judge will be distracted by your beauty.

When you have to testify at your trial, do not let the formality of court scare you. Stand aggressively behind your beliefs, and do not try to control your tone or your temper. If you feel provoked, criticize your spouse. Refuse to use her name and just refer to her as "the crazy ...." The judge will appreciate your candor.

When you are being cross-examined by your spouse's attorneys, you should assert your authority. Interrupt the attorney and speak

Chapter Two: Screwing Up Your Kids While Divorcing

out of turn. Feel free to give them dirty looks, and craft a clever response to any question you find ridiculous. When you've finally had enough, threaten violence. "Your Honor, I've about had it with this guy. If we don't stop now, I'm liable to jump across this courtroom table and deck him." Judges do not condone that kind of chaos in their courtroom, so they will likely let you step down from the witness stand.

Your presence and behavior in court ultimately affects the judge's opinion of you as a parent. If you do not appear, dress, or act respectfully in court, he or she will not get a good impression of you. Your children are also conscious of your actions. If you do not dress appropriately for court, they will not learn that social norms dictate that our attire greatly affect how we are perceived by others, and there are situations where it should reflect a certain respect for authority.

- How To Screw Up Your Children -

- Dress inappropriately for court.

(Your children will believe it is acceptable to behave without regard to circumstances and social norms.)

Time To Get Some Assistance

You do not need to manage your divorce alone. There are special interest groups out there that are more than willing to hold your hand along the way. They will take on your cause, support you throughout your trial, and stop at nothing to get the results they —I mean you—want.

Who are the members of these groups? Some members of these groups lost their own custody cases. Many were judged to be unfit parents, and because they blame everyone but themselves, they have an ax to grind with the legal system. They will channel this resentment into your case and become great advocates for you.

These special interest groups are rigid in their beliefs, and nothing will alter their position. Once they have taken on your case, they will not turn their back on you. They do not worry about abstract concepts such as "innocent until proven guilty," and they only search for the evidence that supports their cause. They passionately believe that any litigant they support - in this case, you - is likely to be the victim of the corrupt legal system, so they will support your allegations against your spouse, no matter how untruthful, slanderous, or ridiculous they may be.

These special interest groups will also be vocal supporters of you in court. They love attention and will show up to your hearings and even picket outside of the courtroom. They may enlist television news reporters who will be willing to cover your case on air. Hopefully, these reporters will be more interested in exploitation and sensationalism than journalistic integrity, and they will present the facts as told to them by your supporters.

If the leaders of these special interest groups think that your case is going south, and you are likely to lose, they will take drastic action. They will accuse the judge of unethical behavior, and they will have your lawyer ask the judge to recuse him or herself from the case. If that does not work, they will use scare tactics. They will flood the phones with anonymous calls, conduct smear campaigns on social media, and make threats to the judges, the witnesses, and the professionals involved in the case. If there are any experts involved, such as child custody evaluators or guardians ad litem, they will accuse these professionals of collusion by implying that your spouse is paying them off for their false testimony. You do realize that some of these things are a bit crazy, but these special interests are willing to do your bidding for you, co-opting your case for their cause. How could you say no?

※ ※ ※

Affiliating yourself with special interest groups can be very dangerous for you and your children. These groups thrive on creating conflict, and they will push you to keep fighting even if it means you lose everything, including your children. They love receiving attention and will try to get as much media coverage as possible though publicizing your case will humiliate your children. These special interest groups also know that sensationalism gets more exposure, so they may try to coerce you and your children into making absurd, unfounded allegations to bring more awareness to their cause. Their perception of your attorney's competence or the testimony of your witnesses may be grossly out of touch with reality, so listening to their opinions can cloud your reasoning. Also, many of these groups are not afraid to try and use intimidation tactics to scare the professionals involved in your litigation into deciding in your favor. Ultimately, associating with these special interests will make you look like a person with very poor judgment.

CHAPTER TWO: SCREWING UP YOUR KIDS WHILE DIVORCING

- How To Screw Up Your Children -

- Let a so-called advocacy group fight for you during your divorce.

(They will look out for their best interest, not the best interest of you or your children.)

- Have your divorce covered by the media.

(Your children will feel humiliated that their family conflict is being broadcast for all to see.)

- Accuse the judge of being corrupt.

(Your children will learn to lie and to be disrespectful toward authority figures.)

Manipulate The Shrink

Do your children need a shrink to help them deal with your impending divorce? Of course they do! If you are going through a contested custody case, taking your children to therapy will make it appear that you are invested in their emotional health. And if the therapist likes you, he or she will be a very strong advocate for your case. This professional's opinion weighs heavily on the court. Sure, there is a chance that your children say something damaging about you to the therapist, but there are things you can do to significantly reduce that risk.

Be the first parent to meet with the counselor so that you could lead with your side of the story. This way the therapist can align with you against your spouse right from the beginning. Blame your husband for the divorce and talk about the entire trauma you and your children have had to endure. In fact, you should meet with the therapist at the beginning of every session to put your personal spin on the events since the last session. Let the therapist know that your spouse has no interest in being involved and should not be included in any sessions. This way there is no chance that he will share his perspective.

On the drive to the therapist's office, you should coach your children on what to say during the session. Remind them of every questionable thing their dad did in the past week. Push them to recall how upset they were and how bad they felt. If you do not have much to go on, just blow things totally out of proportion. This will position the children to speak negatively about their other parent with the counselor. You should also remind them of all the fun you had together. You visited the zoo, went out for a fancy dinner, and watched a *SpongeBob* marathon. You can bet they will share those things with the therapist too.

On the way home from the meeting, grill your children about what they told the therapist. If they said anything bad about you, you do not want to be surprised in court. If your children protest these interrogations, let them know you are just interested in their treatment and want to make sure that they are telling the truth, at least your version of it.

As soon as the contested child custody case is over, be sure to stop the therapy sessions immediately. There was no point in your children meeting with a psychotherapist aside from making you look good in court. That is no longer necessary, and you could find better ways to spend your money. The children probably spent that costly hour playing games or messing around with puppets.

CHAPTER TWO: SCREWING UP YOUR KIDS WHILE DIVORCING

It may be beneficial for your children to get help from a psychotherapist to handle the reality of your divorce. For the treatment to be effective, it is crucial that both parents participate. This allows the therapist to get the most information possible to develop a complete picture of the family and a better understanding of the patient. Providing the psychotherapist with misinformation may result in improper treatment.

Prompting your children to mention your virtues and your spouse's vices to the therapist is a harmful way of manipulating them. It taints your children's memories of the experiences they have with both of their parents. It might also prevent your children from making spontaneous, honest disclosures in therapy. Questioning your children about what was said in the session often has unintended consequences. Your children know what you want to hear, and they will censor what they tell you. You are, in effect, teaching them to lie to you.

Once the divorce is settled, you should not pull your children out of therapy abruptly. Most children develop an attachment to their therapist and losing that support suddenly can be painful for them. The proper way to terminate therapy is to devote the last few sessions to the meaning of the experience and the lessons they learned. This closure allows your children to feel they can trust others, even those they may not see again in the future.

- How To Screw Up Your Children -

- Try to manipulate your children's therapist.

(Biasing your children's therapist could lead to improper treatment.)

- Coach your children to report good things about you and bad things about their other parent in therapy.

(This will also give the therapist an inaccurate picture of the family. Furthermore, it will taint the children's memory of their experiences.)

- Once the legal case is over, abruptly pull your children from therapy.

(Your children will lose an important source of emotional support.)

Exploit Your Spouse's Mental Illness

If your spouse suffers a mental disorder of any kind (and who doesn't these days?), you have won the custody lottery. Of course, if we are talking about a personality disorder, such as Borderline, Antisocial, or Obsessive-Compulsive Personality Disorder, you could assume complete success. Your spouse has a deeply engrained pattern of behavior that impairs how he or she deals with other people, and it will be simple to convince the court that your children will be better off with you. However, if your spouse has ever shown any signs of depression, anxiety, phobias, substance abuse, or an eating disorder, you are also well on your way to winning full custody, and your ex will likely be demoted to noncustodial parent status.

The key to using your spouse's mood and behavior to your benefit is to blow it way out of proportion, so it appears that your spouse suffers from serious mental illness. Has she ever been in a bad mood or had a rough day? Sure she has, it is just a part of life. You can argue in court that your spouse suffers from periods of depression and anxiety. In your mind, if she has ever devoted herself to the Atkins® diet or skipped lunch, she has exhibited signs of an eating disorder. She is a terrible role model for your daughters, and you are fearful that they might develop this illness if she retains custody. Remember those crazy nights in college where he could put away several shots in a row? He is likely to repeat this irresponsible behavior again in the future. You can not have a binge drinker responsible for the wellbeing of your children.

If your spouse has ever seen a mental health professional in any capacity or for any reason, you can find condemning evidence to use in your litigation. If you can not access the actual treatment file, search through the insurance records or payment history until you get what you need. Your spouse was in treatment for a mental disorder and, thus, can not possibly be a decent parent to your children.

Tell your children about their other parent's mental illness in an effort to turn them against him or her. Tell them about the psychotherapists he or she has seen and all of the medicines that were prescribed. Every time your spouse expresses displeasure with you or gets angry, blame it on his or her mental disorder.

* * *

Hearing the sordid details of their parent's mental and emotional problems will make your children anxious. They may begin to fear their parent, and they may worry that they will also develop psychological problems. At the very least, your children will lose respect for their parent, and that relationship will suffer.

When you create a negative stigma around mental health issues, your children are affected by your judgment. They might not be old enough to understand that psychiatric issues run the gamut from mild to severe. In the future, your children may be ashamed if they experience any psychological difficulties. They may refuse to speak to a mental health professional who could help them resolve their problems.

A person can have a mental disorder and still be a highly competent parent. Parental competence is not just defined by the presence or absence of a psychiatric disorder.

- How To Screw Up Your Children -

- Use your spouse's psychotherapy history as a weapon to obtain custody of the children.

(Your children will be separated from a parent they likely love and care for. Furthermore, a visit to a mental health professional does not, by definition, mean that a person has a mental illness that impairs the ability to be a good parent.)

- Exaggerate your spouse's symptoms to make them look extremely disturbed.

(Your children will likely lose respect for their parent, and their relationship will be damaged.)

Con The Child Custody Evaluator

The judge deciding your case is the one who gets to dictate what is in the best interest of your children. However, the judge will often order help obtaining the information he or she needs to make an informed conclusion. A guardian ad litem, (usually an attorney), or a forensic child custody evaluator, (a mental health professional specially trained to evaluate a parent's ability to parent), will be required to investigate the case and submit recommendations to the judge. They focus on each parent's ability to meet their children's needs to determine what is most suitable for the children. Their suggestions usually include which parent should have physical and legal custody, final-decision making, and holidays and summer vacation time. Don't worry if a guardian or child custody evaluator is assigned to your case. He or she is there to document how destructive, inappropriate, and psychologically sick your spouse is. You, of course, will be found to be psychologically healthy and a perfect parent.

During the evaluation, do not ever tell the truth. Have some fun with the examiner, and see if you can pull the wool over his or her eyes. These professionals are humorously naïve and will fall for any good story you have. They love allegations, so make many about your spouse. Make sure some are specific to your spouse's emotional functioning, substance abuse, and morally questionable behavior. When you make up allegations, the professional will pour plenty of time and effort into tracking down their veracity and less time analyzing you.

When the professional comes to visit at your house, your home should look like a spread in *Martha Stewart Living*. Everything should be impeccable; there should not be a speck of dirt on the floor, a bit of dust on the furniture, or a crease in any of the bed linens. Arrange a bouquet of tulips in the front entry and a bowl of fresh fruit on the kitchen counter for effect, and light vanilla candles in all of the bathrooms.

While giving the house tour, you want to put the evaluator in a good mood. Tell her how much you love her dress even if it looks like a sack of potatoes, and compliment her haircut even if seems she hasn't brushed it. A little flattery could go a long way. Your goal is to make the evaluator like you.

It is also clever to stage your home with examples of your superior parenting skills. Display a half-finished art project in the den to show how you and the children are creative together on the weekends. Once the evaluator leaves, you could throw the eyesore in the trash. You certainly don't want your children to expect you to undertake such time-wasting, pointless projects in the future. Don't forget to set a plate of fresh-baked chocolate chip cookies on the dining table and mention how your children love to help you in the kitchen. Realtors do it for open houses, so why wouldn't you for such an important home visit? Leave textbooks out on the dining room table. Tell the Guardian you were just reviewing a homework assignment with the children, and you did not have a chance to put away the textbooks. Finally, stock the

CHAPTER TWO: SCREWING UP YOUR KIDS WHILE DIVORCING

pantry with rice cakes and dried fruit, and toss the Doritos and the beef jerky in the high cabinet above the refrigerator.

While engaged in conversation about your children, slip in some criticisms of your ex. You could touch on how he drops the children off late to school or how he never checks their homework. You should also make allegations regarding his poor mental health, substance abuse, and questionable morals. Make him sound incompetent.

The impact on the evaluator will be tenfold if they hear the same information from your children. Kids are just so believable. Prompt yours to mention the failings and misdeeds of their other parent. Just before the professional's visit, remind your children of all of the times their dad served them Pop-Tarts® for breakfast or let them watch a gory, R-rated movie before bedtime that gave them nightmares. Do not forget to recap all the reasons they dislike their father's new girlfriend. There is a good chance your children will mention these things to the evaluator. It would also be helpful if your children made you sound even better to the guardian than you already are. Tell your teenagers that if you get custody, they get a new car. They will have nothing bad to say about you.

***

In contested child custody cases, the court selects the custodial parent by carefully considering the best interest of the child. Some of these factors pertain to the children. Are the children more attached to one parent? Do any of the children have medical problems, educational difficulties, or mental illnesses? Other factors have to do with the parents' ability to meet the children's needs. Is either parent suffering from a mental disorder? Does either have a drug or alcohol problem? What is the parent's ability to facilitate a relationship between the children and their other parent? What are the parent's emotional and economic resources? An evaluator's job is to determine the answers to these questions.

Unless you are dealing with a new, inexperienced guardian or child custody evaluator, attempts to manipulate him, or her will not work. The burning candles, freshly baked cookies, and flattery will not fool the professional. Experienced evaluators are trained to see through the guise, and they are used to parents trying to deceive them into order to win a more favorable custody arrangement.

More importantly, your attempt to deceive the evaluator will actually hurt your children. When you lie to the guardian or child custody evaluator, your children realize what you are telling these professionals do not match up with their reality. They know you are being dishonest and will likely lose respect for you. They are also learning that

Chapter Two: Screwing Up Your Kids While Divorcing

it is acceptable to lie, even to the court. When you stage a show for the evaluator, your children get high hopes that the behavior will continue. They will be disappointed when the evaluator leaves and things go back to normal.

Manipulating your children to speak ill of their other parent is very damaging. When children remember only their negative experiences, it alters their sense of reality. When they mention these distortions repeatedly, it can change their memory. When they look back, your children will remember their other parent as very flawed when that might be far from the truth.

- How To Screw Up Your Children -

- Make unfounded allegations about your spouse.

(Your children will be angry that you are fabricating stories about their other parent.)

- Clean and organize the house prior to a home visit from the guardian ad litem or child custody evaluator.

(The children will realize you have no problem presenting a phony front to other people.)

- Prompt your children to lie to the evaluator or guardian.

(Your children will learn that it is acceptable to lie.)

Lean On Your Children

Going through a divorce is emotionally exhausting. Parenting children while divorcing, next to impossible. Sure, you could help yourself get healthier by exercising, reading books, playing sports, and learning to meditate, but that all seems like too much work. You do not want to handle it alone, and you need some support. Unfortunately, your family and friends have gotten tired of your complaints, and you don't feel like wasting money for a therapist. It is time to get some comfort from the only people who love you unconditionally, your children.

It is no fun eating dinner alone while your children are out chasing their dreams, or sitting around guessing *Jeopardy* questions in an empty room. You want your children around more often to keep you company so that you do not get bored or feel lonely. You must get your children to run home to you every day after school, and you can do so by discouraging them from doing the things that take them away from you. Undermine their confidence in their extracurricular activities, like running track, arguing on the debate team, or acting in drama club productions. Remind them that there are better athletes, debaters, and actors in their class, and there is no point in joining track, trying out for the debate team, or auditioning for the school play. Watch how quickly they lose interest in those activities.

To keep them home on weekends, you must sabotage their social lives. Otherwise, they might spend time out at football games, attending parties, or going on dates, and you'll be abandoned. Tell your daughters that the boys in their class only want to date the cooler, more attractive girls, and tell your sons that they can not compete with the popular jocks. There is no sense even making an effort. On top of that, let your children know that their friends can not be trusted because at some point, these people will likely betray them. You are the only one who will always be there for them. It is you together versus the world.

If tearing down your children's confidence does not work, scare them senseless. Raise concerns about the safety of the fun things they want to do. If they want to spend the night at a friend's house, suggest that the father seems creepy or that the mother is crazy, and, for their protection, they probably should not go. Eventually, your children will stop asking to stay at their friends' homes during your parenting time, and your work is done.

Make sure to create the same expectation of fear regarding your ex. Before the children leave to stay with their father, in a loving, concerned manner say, "I'm sure you will have a good time, but if you are scared, if you miss me, if you feel ignored, or if he mistreats you, call me, and I will come get you."

If all of the above efforts fail, you have no choice but to turn up the drama to create a little separation anxiety. Tell your children how lonely you feel when they are not with you and how much you are suffering. Let them see your tears when they leave the house. Tell them how much you need them; you need them more than their friends do, and you especially need them more than their other parent does. Tell them you don't feel appreciated. Life is short and in the blink of an eye, something tragic can happen that would take you away from them forever. Cue the scary music.

* * *

It is not healthy for your children to feel responsible for your happiness and wellbeing. Children become parentified when they are obligated to take on the physical and emotional needs of their parents. This role reversal requires children to shoulder adult responsibilities that overburden them.

If you destroy your children's confidence in the things that take them away from you, your relationship will become codependent. Your children will become extremely insecure and will prefer the safety of caring for you over other, healthier options. They will not want to be involved in extracurricular or social activities, and they will be afraid to try new things. This will inhibit your children's growth, sense of competence, psychological development, and independence.

Undermining your children's relationships with others to keep them close to you will damage them. If you discourage your children from

Chapter Two: Screwing Up Your Kids While Divorcing

building friendships, they will not have appropriate peer relationships or develop confidantes. Ultimately, they will not learn to trust other people. If you create the expectation of fear in your children by being overly concerned for their safety in other people's homes, they will be scared to go anywhere. They might even be afraid to spend time with their other parent.

Nobody said that parenting is easy. It is very difficult to stay sane under the stress of a divorce and the pressure of raising children. But you must nurture yourself, and if you need extra support turn to friends, family, a therapist, or a support group. Do not turn to your children for help.

- How To Screw Up Your Children -

- **Look to your children for your emotional support.**

(This will make your children feel responsible for how you feel, which will burden them.)

- **Discourage your children from spending time away from you.**

(You will develop an unhealthy codependent relationship.)

- **Let your children know how upset you will be when they are with your ex.**

(Your children will feel guilty for enjoying their time with their other parent.)

Chapter Three: Screwing Up Co-Parenting

Make Your Child Your Messenger

Your children go back and forth between the two homes, so why not make them your personal messengers and have them communicate with your ex for you? This seems perfect. You will create a buffer between you and your ex, and you will no longer have to worry about saying the wrong thing, controlling your volume, or hearing her annoying voice during your children's transitions. You can also eliminate the uncomfortable phone calls, rambling texts, and long written notes.

Just tell your children what you want to say to your ex, and they will relay the message. "Tell your mother the child support check will be late." It is done, and you did not have to endure a lecture. If you have your children tell her, "Dad is picking us up on Saturday morning instead of Friday night," you do not have to hear her mumble under her breath. And you can even have your children bring you the answers to everyday questions if you tell them to "Ask your mother if she's seen your black sweater." It's like having a personal emissary who engages in shuttle diplomacy between the two homes. Sure, the message might get lost in translation,

Chapter Three: Screwing Up Co-Parenting

but that is your ex's problem to resolve. Your life will be much easier.

Have your children hand-deliver your child support and alimony checks to your ex. Since children do not have a realistic monetary sense, they will think you are giving an extraordinary amount, and will believe you are extremely generous to their mother. If your ex complains about the children seeing the check, put it in an envelope, but do not seal the envelope entirely. This way your kids could easily peek inside to see the amount written on the check. Just think of the fortune you will save on postage.

Mental health professionals use the term triangulation to describe a situation where two family members, in this case, the parents, will not communicate directly with each other, and instead correspond through

a third party, their children. It forces the children to become a part of a triangle and places them in the middle of their parents' conflict. Your children do not want to be used as an intermediary or put in the center of communications between you and your ex, because it causes anxiety. They are caught in a loyalty bind between their parents, inadvertently exposed to their parents' emotional reactions to the messages, and given the burden of relaying the correct information promptly. They may even feel responsible for the outcome of their parents' fights.

When you use your children as messengers, you are also teaching them that it is acceptable to avoid direct communication and instead correspond via a third party. These poor communication skills will damage their personal relationships throughout their lives.

Communicating with your ex may not be easy, but it is your responsibility. There are measures that you can take to prevent conflict. Speak politely to your ex, make requests rather than statements, and keep the conversation about the children. If you can not engage in conversation with your ex without it turning explosive, send an email, write a text message, or drop a note in the mailbox. And, instead of using your children to deliver checks, send the money directly from the bank.

- How To Screw Up Your Children -

- Have your children relay messages between you and your ex.

(Your children will learn it is acceptable to avoid direct communication and communicate through a third party.)

- Have your children serve as couriers for the checks and documents sent between the two homes.

(Your children will feel stuck in the middle of their parents' conflict and responsible their parents' communications with each other.)

CHAPTER THREE: SCREWING UP CO-PARENTING

Conduct Interrogations

If you have ever seen an episode of *Law and Order* (and who hasn't), you've seen FBI agents, police detectives, private eyes, and news reporters pressure witnesses for information. Why shouldn't you? After a weekend with your ex, your children return with all the intelligence you need. You must give them the 3rd degree, and extract all the knowledge from them that you can.

Ask your children for a play-by-play of how they spent their time at their mother's home. You could press them for details about what they did for entertainment, what they ate, where they went, what time they came home, and what time they went to sleep. More importantly, ask your children what your ex was up to, whom she was out with, and who visited the home. "Was it the bodybuilder with the fake tan? You could tell me." Find out what they think about your ex's rebound, and be sure to get a sense from the children about your ex's mood and how she is coping with the divorce. You might ask, "Does she miss me? Did she ask if I'm dating anyone?" Inquire about other specifics that are also not any of your business, like the progress on her kitchen remodel, new purchases made for the home, and the price tag of the shiny convertible now parked in her driveway. Use the children as spies embedded behind enemy lines.

It would also be extremely helpful if you could get your children to snoop around for documents that can prove useful to you if you were ever to return to court. Have them text you pictures of personal letters, assorted bills, legal papers, and other records they find lying around the house. Reward your children's efforts to steal valuable information on the other parent's computer, like emails and word documents. Just cross your fingers that they don't become double agents.

It is natural to be curious about what goes on in your ex's home, but be careful not to interrogate your children after they return from a visit with their other parent. Doing so places them in the middle of the conflict between you and your ex, and forces them to choose between their parents. To stay loyal to you, they must betray their other parent, and if they keep your ex's confidence, they anger you. Either way they lose.

When you pressure your children for information, you also violate their need for privacy. It is important for them to have their own space, and the time they spend with their other parent should be free from anxiety and criticism. It is ok to ask general questions like "Did you have a nice weekend?" However, do not push any further. If they want to share any more details with you, they will do it on their own. Remember, as long as your children are not at risk, how or with whom your ex spends his or her free time is no longer your business.

Definitely do not have your children spy on your ex. If the information they provide is used in any way against their other parent, your children will feel responsible for the outcome of the divorce or custody dispute. They will feel guilty for supplying the evidence, and it is an unfair burden for them to carry.

Chapter Three: Screwing Up Co-Parenting

- How To Screw Up Your Children -

- Interrogate your children after every stay with their other parent.

(This will violate their need for privacy, and they will feel anxious every time they transition back to your household.)

- Pressure your children to snoop around your ex's house for information that can benefit you in future litigation.

(Your children will feel guilty for betraying their other parent's trust.)

Create Uneasy Transitions

Transitioning the children from one home to the other is an excellent time to escalate the conflict with your ex and the perfect opportunity to add tension to an already stressful situation. If you can design these moves to be seamless for you and miserable for everyone else, they are bound to screw up your children. So here's the plan...

Start by ensuring that your children's transitions are chaotic and unpredictable. Veer from the parenting plan, revolve the schedule around your ever-changing social calendar, and don't ever let your children know the plans in advance or they might have time to prepare. "Surprise! You're going to Mom's today." A few minutes before you must leave, throw some of their stuff in a bag without bothering to ask them what they will need with them for the visit.

Make sure the pick up and drop off times suit only your schedule. Don't consider what works best for your children, after school for example, and certainly do not pick a time that makes your ex's life easier. In fact, the only times you are available, coincidently, are the same times as her usual tennis match or weekly manicure. Then show up late without calling first. That will really infuriate her.

If you want to really mess with your children, spend a portion of the transition time criticizing your ex. Call out her bad haircut and the extra few pounds she's carrying around, or condemn her for feeding the children too much fast-food. It is a great opportunity for you because you are face to face with your ex and your children can witness your judgment on her decision-making. Keep the conflict going!

Spend the rest of the time arguing about your parenting plan. Remind your ex-spouse about any event in the upcoming weeks you know she can't attend, and insist she cover for you next Monday night because you prefer watching football with the guys to babysitting. Finally, ask her for a detailed breakdown of how she used the last child support check, and then nitpick every expense within earshot of the kids. Berate her for squandering the money that is for the children.

If you want to turn it up a notch, bring other people along for the ride. The more people involved, the greater chance for a good fight, so invite your children's friends or bring along last night's date. Finally, if you just feel you have not screwed up your children enough, insist that the transfers take place in the parking lot of the nearest police station. Nothing makes your ex look crazier than alleging that cops need to supervise these transitions. It's just a lucky coincidence the station is also ten minutes closer to your home.

Important note: If you succeed in causing your ex to unwind, make sure to capture all of the drama. Take photos! Better yet, take videos. Continue to provoke her into doing or saying things that make her look unstable. (Get a close-up of her giving you the finger while she drives off without a seatbelt.) Save all evidence for future litigation, and show it to the child custody evaluator, guardian ad litem, and the judge. Heck, share it with anyone who thinks your ex is sane.

Your children experience a great deal of stress shuffling back and forth from one parent to the other, so it is important that you make these transitions as smooth as possible for them. Establish and stick to a schedule, and share that schedule with your children so that they can anticipate the change. Being prepared could also minimize their stress, so make sure that each house has adequate clothes, toiletries, toys, books, etc. Children need to have space in both homes that is comfortable and welcoming, and because they crave consistency, routines like mealtime, homework time, and bedtime should remain the same. When your children return to your home, you must give them time to adjust. Engage in a quiet activity or establish a ritual with them, like eating pizza for dinner, so they know what to expect when they arrive.

Any conflict between you and your ex during this transition time only heightens your children's anxiety. Do not argue with your ex, and do not use this time to discuss arrangements for the children. Instead, be cordial and focus on the task at hand, transitioning your children. Also, refrain from including a third party or taking videos, which only makes the experience more stressful for your kids. Finally, if your relationship is so volatile that law enforcement need to supervise the transitions, your children are likely terrified that something terrible is bound to happen during this time, so only resort to supervised transitions if it is necessary.

- How To Screw Up Your Children -

- Cause conflict with your ex during your children's transitions from one household to the other.

(You are adding more stress to an already tense situation.)

- Record these transitions.

(Your children will feel that you are invading their privacy, and they will be angry with you for behaving inappropriately.)

- Make untrue allegations that your ex is abusive to you during transitions.

(Your children will learn that it is acceptable to lie when it serves their goals.)

Be Selfish

Do not ever let your children take toys, clothes, or personal items from your home to your ex's place. The stuff in your house is yours. Period. This includes, but is not limited to; American Girl® dolls, FIFA 16 for Xbox®, the new Peyton Manning jersey you bought your son at the mall, old ice-skates, and the copy of *Harry Potter and the Sorcerer's Stone* on the shelf in the library. If they need this stuff so badly when they are visiting your ex, let their father buy them a duplicate to keep at his home. Also, make it clear that the stuff from your ex's home is never to find its way through your front door.

Check your children's suitcases and backpacks to make sure they are not trying to smuggle any of "mom's" things to their father's home, and conduct the same inspection when they return to assure they have not brought any of "dad's" tainted things back with them. If you find contraband, return it immediately. This reinforces the rule that the children are not to move their possessions from one house to the other and will serve to remind your ex to keep his belongings to himself. It is important to maintain boundaries, after all.

Remember that the same edict applies to gifts received from extended family. Do not let anything from your ex's parents into your house. The only acceptable gifts to remain in your home are from your side of the family.

* * *

Do not use your children's personal possessions as a way to escalate the conflict between you and your ex. When you forbid your children to move their stuff between your home and your ex's home, you deny your children the comfort that comes with having the things they enjoy with them during difficult transitions. Your children will be humiliated if they must go through inspections to ensure they are following the rules. Additionally, your children will never feel at home in either household. They will feel that everything is either Mom's or Dad's and will never feel anything belongs to them.

- How To Screw Up Your Children -

- Do not allow your children to take any of their personal possessions to their other parent's home.

(Your children will feel that everything, including the homes they live in, belongs to mom or dad and nothing is theirs.)

- Do not allow your children to bring any of their toys, books, or clothing from their other parent's home to yours.

(Your children will feel frustrated that they can not do as they wish with their things.)

Mess With Phone Calls, Video Chats, Texts, And Emails

Today, people are expected to be available twenty-four/seven via cell phones, texts, tablets, and emails. You long for the time when you could spend the day on your own, without interference via technology. You, a wonderful parent, want your children to experience life without such intrusions.

When your ex-wife calls to speak with the children, tell her they are busy studying and then need to shower and get to bed. Let her know they just can not return her call that day. Control the cell phone plan so you can put restrictions on what time the children can receive phone calls or texts. This procedure will effectively block your ex-wife from daily contact with your kids. If your ex-wife accuses you of gatekeeping, explain that you are just trying to make sure the children get their studying in and their homework done before bedtime.

Email and texts are free methods to taunt, intimidate, infuriate, and control your ex-spouse. Since it doesn't yet cost a cent to send one email or a thousand, bombard your ex-wife with emails. In each message, highlight one behavior that either she or the children exhibit that is of concern to you and would, therefore, likely be of concern to a judge. Follow the email up with a critique, not only of your ex-wife's behavior, but also her motivation. Don't hesitate to send multiple follow-up emails expounding on what you think the motivations are for her conduct. Be sure to imply sinister, self-serving motives to everything she does. Always finish the email with a sentence or two about how her behavior is not in the children's best interest.

When your ex-wife reads the email or text, she might mutter a comment or sneer. If the children are present, they are likely to hear the contents of the email or text communication directly from their mother. This strategy is ingenious since it places the children in the middle of the conflict without you even being present.

Use big, powerful words in your communications. Allege that your ex-wife's behavior is "egregious," "beyond reproach," and "reprehensible." Nothing should ever be "somewhat" or "occasionally." It should be "always" or "constantly." Be active in your writing. Don't allow room for exceptions. Let your ex-wife know that she always engages in this disturbing behavior and that it is damaging to the children's mental health. Remind your ex-wife that her behavior will leave a lifelong scar that will prevent your kids from having healthy, happy lives.

Much like being fashionably late to a party, when your ex-wife contacts you, delay your responses. You are busy, aren't you? Surely you haven't time to constantly check your email inbox or incoming texts. Even if you do, she doesn't have to know. Delayed responding will frustrate her, and she will possibly complain later to the children that you never respond to her emails. Later, you can let the children know that you are busy trying to make a living to support them and their mother financially. Tell them you don't have time to check your email all the time. The children will then try to convince their mother that you don't always respond because you are attempting to provide for their

CHAPTER THREE: SCREWING UP CO-PARENTING

needs. You will look good to your children and will irritate their mom.

You can frustrate and anger your ex-wife by delaying a response when there is a looming deadline, such as a RSVP for an event or submission of an application for an activity. Let her sweat it out, wondering if you will or will not accommodate her request. Respond at the last possible minute. If the children complain to you that you waited too long to reply, let them know that even though you are busy, you will always make time for important decisions regarding their needs.

Blocking phone calls between your ex-spouse and the children is not good for the kids. This behavior is one of many gatekeeping behaviors that will negatively affect your children. Research has shown that children's feeling they have easy access to both parents is crucial for the overall mental health of children of divorce.

Delayed responses to reasonable emails and texts between parents can be detrimental to children. When the delay's goal is to upset the other parent, that anger and frustration will trickle down to the kids. This delay tactic, once again, places the children back in the middle of their parents' conflicts.

Using email and texts to harass the other parent is also indirectly bad for your kids. Anything that damages the relationship between the parents will ultimately destroy the co-parenting abilities of the parents. Poor co-parenting will then cause problems for the children.

- How To Screw Up Your Children -

- Restrict your ex from easy phone access to the children.

(This will teach your children that it is okay to hurt another person by restricting access to his or her children.)

- Use emails and texts to harass your ex-spouse.

(Your children will undoubtedly hear about your hostile emails and texts and lose respect for you.)

- Do not respond quickly to an email requesting information from your ex-spouse.

(Your children will be left to wonder if there is a resolution to a situation that requires both of their parents' response.)

CHAPTER THREE: SCREWING UP CO-PARENTING

Ruin Holidays And Summer Vacations

Even if you failed to receive sole custody or final decision-making, you could still effectively screw up your children by creating conflict over what parenting time you do have. When it comes to holidays and summer vacations, divorce settlements typically dictate which parent gets to share time with their children, and you will be fighting for ALL holidays and summertime vacations. Even if your attorney recommends alternating the holidays annually with your ex, do not step down. You are the noncustodial parent, and you have less parenting time during the year. You deserve more! Also, your children probably prefer to be with you during their time off.

Regardless of how observant you are, insist on getting the children for even the most obscure religious holidays. If you are Catholic, demand the children be with you on all of the Holy Days of Obligation. If you are Jewish, insist on celebrating Shemini Atzeret and Lag B'Omer together. No one will question you on matters of religion, so this is a great tactic to get extra parenting time. If you do not have a clue as to what the holiday is about, look to Google for a simple explanation that you could share with your children.

All holidays are important, but it is especially critical that you push for the holidays that are most important to your ex. If her favorite thing is watching the children hunt for Easter eggs, fight hard to get the children on Easter. This will cause major conflict, and it will infuriate your ex. Your righteous payback is making the holidays a source of pain for her.

If you have custody of the children on holidays, it is totally fine to surrender it to your ex if you receive a better invitation. Maybe your new girlfriend invites you to ski the French Alps over Christmas. How can you miss that? Just throw out some excuse, and drop your children's presents off on your way to the airport. There is always next year. If the custody agreement orders you to share custody over their holiday breaks, schedule the transitions on the actual holiday so you can destroy everyone's good cheer. Make last-minute changes, and cause your ex and her family and friends to scramble to adjust their plans.

In addition to holidays, demand that you get your children for their entire summer vacation. You will have their undivided attention for several weeks in a row, which gives you plenty of time to implement your campaign of denigration against your ex. Use every opportunity you have to badmouth her, and isolate the children from their mother when they are yours. If you are busy with work, hire a nanny or ask a relative to care for the children—do not let their mother pitch in and help.

It is during these holidays and summer vacations that you have a chance to gain an advantage over your ex by taking your children on extravagant vacations. If she does not have the means to do the same herself, this is an extremely effective way of upsetting her. You know your children will rave about their trip to St. Tropez, but make sure your ex sees all of the fun you have by posting the family vacation photos all over social media. You should also buy your children a few souvenirs to bring back home with them so they can remind your ex of what she missed every time she goes into their rooms.

***

CHAPTER THREE: SCREWING UP CO-PARENTING

Fighting for all holidays and vacations is another way to antagonize your ex-spouse and expose your children to more conflict. It also deprives your children of enjoying some of the holidays with their other parent. If you do share holidays with your ex, and you create tension on the holidays by delaying transitions, it will cause your children additional stress. Finally, your children will miss their other parent and might become sad, frustrated, and withdrawn when you restrict their access during holidays breaks and summer vacations. These holiday times and vacations should be happy memories for your children, do not take that away from them.

- How To Screw Up Your Children -

- Insist on getting your children for every holiday.

(Your children will be frustrated that they have to miss special holiday celebrations with their other parent.)

- Make last-minute schedule changes on holidays to mess with your ex's holiday plans.

(Your conflict will put stress on your children and will take the joy out of their holiday.)

- Isolate the children from their other parent while they are with you for extended summer vacation time.

(Your children will feel trapped, and they will miss their other parent during this time.)

Have Different Rules At Each Home

If you discipline the same way your ex does, you can lose an important advantage with your children. If you want them to like you, you must always play the good-guy. Model your behavior after Mr. and Mrs. Bueller, whose son Ferris never managed to get in trouble, or the parents of the spoiled teenagers on the MTV show *My Super Sweet Sixteen*.

Do not force your children to clean up their toys or go to bed until they tell you they are ready to do so. Give into their impulses and tantrums and bribe them with toys and food. "Cookies before dinnertime? Sure, what the heck. Have two." Be the parent who never stays mad for long. If you put a child in time-out, let them out early, and if they have not done what you asked of them, just let it go. Eliminate your teenagers' curfews and do away with other rules in the house such as making beds, emptying the dishwasher, or taking out the trash. In fact, let them do whatever makes them happy. Sure, you are their mother, but first and foremost you are their best friend.

Let your ex be the bad-guy and dole out punishment. Let their father make them do their homework, take out the garbage, and

CHAPTER THREE: SCREWING UP CO-PARENTING

teach them table manners. After your ex doles out the punishment, undermine his parenting by letting them off the hook and coddling them as if they have been victimized. Now is also a great time to spoil them with expensive gifts. Your children will think of you as warm and loving, and they will see your ex as strict, rigid, impatient, and demanding. You will certainly be the favored parent.

Discipline should be consistent in both parents' homes, as this is necessary for children to feel safe and secure. The basic rules in the homes should remain the same, so your children are not confused. While every rule might vary slightly, suitable discipline practiced by both parents will teach children appropriate behavior and self-control.

Most parents discipline their children using one of the four basic styles. On one end of the spectrum is neglectful parenting. These parents are detached, and often minimally involved with their children. Their children are prone to antisocial behavior, have the lowest academic success rate, and the highest level of psychopathology.

Authoritarian parents have extremely high expectations. They believe there is one way to do things, their way. These parents demand blind obedience and their discipline is harsh and punitive. Children who experience this type of discipline fail to learn independent thinking, are more likely to engage in risky behavior, and often have behavioral problems.

Indulgent parents are persistently lenient and practice inconsistent discipline. This style of parenting seems to be very popular among parents who are raising children today. Their children become spoiled, feel entitled, and act impulsively. Often one parent will be more lenient or indulgent in an attempt to be more likable, but when you undermine your ex-spouse's discipline, you are actually doing your children a disservice. They fail to learn the connection between effort and reward, self-control, and appropriate behavior.

The final style is authoritative parenting. These parents exhibit consistency with their discipline, yet do so in a nurturing manner. They explain the rules and use reason to instruct their children. These children learn self-regulation and appropriate social behavior, have the highest levels of academic achievement, and exhibit the lowest levels of problematic behavior. Practicing authoritative parenting will be the healthiest for your children, regardless of the style of discipline practiced by their other parent.

- How To Screw Up Your Children -

- Do not agree to have the same rules at your house as at your ex-spouse's houses.

(When there are two different sets of rules for them to follow, your children will be confused and stressed.)

- Undermine your ex's discipline by coddling your children soon after your ex has punished them.

(Your children will rely on you to absolve them of punishment they deserve, and they will not learn discipline and self-control.)

Don't Be Flexible

Experts say that flexibility is an essential ingredient to successful co-parenting after a divorce. Do not subscribe to this concept, because it does not apply to you. Instead, stand firm on every issue laid out in the court-ordered parenting plan. Be rigid, restrictive, and vindictive.

If your ex is scheduled to pick up the children at 9:00 am, by 9:01 am it is too late. Bumper to bumper traffic, a late start, or maybe a tornado ripped through the center of town— you are not accepting any of those excuses. Better luck next time!

If you give an inch, your ex will take a mile. First it will be last minute courtside seats to a Hawks game on your night, a family reunion planned on your weekend, or attendance at a father-daughter dance. Who knows what will happen next. Succumb to just one request, and you will find yourself on a slippery slope.

You are sticking strictly to the parenting plan, and providing your children with stability and predictability they need. If you change the schedule just once, who knows how it will destroy their psychological development. It is better to be unyielding and hostile toward your ex.

When you are rigid and inflexible, it is harmful to your kids. There will be many exciting opportunities for your children that will not coincide with the court-ordered parenting plan. If you are unwilling to be flexible, they will miss out. Your children will be angry and resent you for these restrictions, and they will feel sad that they are not able to have fun at special events because of their parents' inability to work with each other.

If you are accommodating, your children will have a chance to engage in interesting and fun activities regardless of whose parenting time it is. Making a few exceptions to the parenting plan will not harm their need for predictability. In fact, it will show your children the importance of being flexible and agreeable in relationships with others. Doing the right thing also illustrates to them that their happiness is more important to you than your revenge.

CHAPTER THREE: SCREWING UP CO-PARENTING

- How To Screw Up Your Children -

- Do not be flexible when it comes to any request from your ex.

(This will teach your children to be rigid and unyielding in their future relationships.)

- Ignore your children's requests to deviate from the planned schedule.

(Your children will feel frustrated that they are missing great opportunities simply because those things involve their other parent.)

Point Out Your Ex's Parenting Mistakes

You never make parenting mistakes. Your ex-spouse though, that is another story. What a complete idiot!

Who doesn't know how to log onto the school website? How difficult could it be to sign the children up for fall soccer? And why it is so hard to make it to school pickup on time? It does not take a rocket scientist to figure out these things. They are so simple, but for some reason she can not seem to get them right.

Make sure your children know how often their mother errs. This way they will understand how flawed your ex-spouse is at parenting (among other things, of course). In this area everything is black and white; you're either a good parent or you're not, and your ex is clearly not. If your children are ever uncertain, just recall the time she forgot to turn off the oven. Your children should always follow your direction because you are clearly the better parent.

It is vital to document all of your ex's screw-ups, big or small. (This will be crucial should there ever be a contempt or custody modification action against you.) Use video and audio-recordings, and keep evidence of email exchanges and crazy text messages. Create a master list:

1. Friday, July 22nd, 8:15 am... she gave the children donuts and orange juice for breakfast.

2. Friday, July 22nd, 10:30 am... she dropped off the children for camp 10 minutes late.

3. Friday, July 22nd, 10:00 pm... she neglected to have the children call me.

4. Saturday, July 23rd, 8:15 pm... she let the children stay up 15 minutes past their bedtime.

Do not hesitate to toot your own horn. You dropped off cupcakes at school for the kids' birthdays and once volunteered at the PTA book sale. You are parent-of-the-year!

* * *

CHAPTER THREE: SCREWING UP CO-PARENTING

It is harmful for your children to hear you criticize all of their other parent's mistakes. This critique is just another form of badmouthing your ex, and it will cause your children to lose respect for their other parent or to see you as a bully who is out to humiliate their other parent. Your children are left viewing one or both of their parents as seriously flawed in either scenario, and this is particularly damaging to children because they partially develop their self-image by internalizing their beliefs about their parents. If you are flawed, or your ex is flawed, it is reasonable for them to conclude they must be flawed too. This is not exactly the best way to develop their self-esteem.

- How To Screw Up Your Children -

- Point out all of your ex-spouse's parenting mistakes.

(Your children may begin to see one or both of their parents as flawed and therefore see themselves - an extension of their parents - as flawed as well.)

- Document all of your ex's errors, no matter how trivial.

(When your children are in adult relationships, they will obsess about every little mistake their partner makes.)

Relocate

Moving away with your children is an excellent way to show your ex who's boss. The farther away you go, the better. You will still receive child support and possibly alimony without having to deal with your ex on a regular basis or have him interfere with your life. Just think about you. You could live in an adorable beach bungalow in Malibu, and northeastern winters will be a thing of your past. Sure, it will be harder for your ex to see his children, but that's what FaceTime is for.

Stability and predictability are highly overrated. You want adventure and excitement, and you want your chance to start fresh. If you feel this way, your children will too. They will get to experience a different school, make all new friends, and construct a new image. Your daughter could be just like Tai in *Clueless*, and Alicia Silverstone will take her under her wing and make her part of the in-crowd. But if your ungrateful children complain about having to begin anew on the West Coast, remind them that friends come and go, but you will be in their lives forever.

Your children may also make a big deal about leaving all of their extra-curricular activities behind. Waah-waah-waah! It is no big loss; they were never that great to begin with. If your son plays baseball, tell him there isn't a chance he'll be warming the bench in the Red Sox dugout anytime soon. He can barely catch the ball. If your daughter does not want to leave her cheerleading squad, let her know she is not one of the fittest or most coordinated girls in her high school. She will likely lose her spot to a prettier freshman in the coming years.

Moving to a new location may benefit the custodial parent, but it is rarely best for the children. Relocation increases uncertainty and disrupts the sense of stability that is so important for children during and after divorce. It also tests the relationship between the children and their noncustodial parent by almost eliminating the day-to-day involvement of that parent in their children's lives. Research shows that

as the distance from the custodial parent to the noncustodial parent increases, so does the probability that parent will lose meaningful contact with their children.

There are two times in children's lives when moving is most detrimental. The first is when the child is very young. Moving at that stage of development will upset their attachment to their non-custodial parent. This disruption will have lifelong negative implications for your children. Their relationship with the non-custodial parent may never develop, or it may be grossly impaired. Eventually, that parent might become little more than a stranger to them, and this loss will gravely affect their future relationships.

It is also very difficult to relocate teenagers. In addition to daily contact with one of their parents, they will lose their entire social support system. Teenagers have an intense bond to their friends and their community. They will feel a tremendous loss if they are forced to move away from their network of friends, teachers, and coaches and give up the sports, clubs, school events, and community activities that are an important part of their identity.

- How To Screw Up Your Children -

- Move the children far away from your ex.

(This will disrupt the regular visits the children have with their other parent, and they will lose the benefit of having both parents involved in their day-to-day life.)

- Make the move when your children are very young.

(This may destroy the attachment between your children and their other parent.)

- Make another move when your children are teenagers.

(This removes your children from their entire social support system and all of the school and community activities they engage in.)

Abandon Your Children

When the responsibilities of being a parent get to be too much, just abandon your children. This is the easiest way to avoid the hassles of carpooling, standing out in the cold watching soccer games, or having an uncomfortable conversation with them about the birds and the bees. Besides, your children live with their mother, so you don't really matter that much anyway.

If you are the noncustodial parent, you don't have to quit parenting cold turkey. You can just gradually ease out of your children's lives. Simply follow the plan below:

Step 1: Arrive late for visits and return the children early to your ex.

Step 2: Skip out on your children's extra-curricular activities, and do something better with your time. They will get accustomed to not having your support at their events, and will start to get the hint that you are not that interested in them.

Step 3: Make promises that you never intend to keep. Vow to your children that you will take them on fancy vacations and to lots of amusement parks. Never follow through. After a while, your children will get used to the disappointment, and will learn they can not count on you.

Step 4: Cancel your visits entirely. Canceling last minute is best, because it is especially crushing. You could use any variety of excuses for cancelling, an important meeting you don't want to miss, last minute concert tickets, or maybe you just don't feel like getting off the couch. Any of these will equally screw up your children.

If you want to stay in touch, just do it over the phone. A phone call or a text is just as good as a visit, right? It is a quick and convenient way to keep you up to date on the highlights of your children's lives. Most of their day-to-day stuff is pretty mundane anyway. *Tip: Want to keep your calls brief? Call when your children are busy with homework or getting ready for bed.

If anyone confronts you about reneging on your obligation to be a parent, blame your ex. After all, she fought for primary custody, and she is a real pain in the neck to deal with on a regular basis. Just lie to your children, and tell them their mother prevented you from seeing them more often. Let them know that if it were not for their mother, you would be very involved in their lives.

Many parents have skipped out on their kids only to be welcomed back later. Hugh Jackman, the esteemed actor, had a mother who abandoned him. Later in life, his mother reappeared, and he welcomed her back with open arms. You can reap the benefits of having children at a time in your life that is more convenient for you without any of the daily hassles of being a parent. Plus, during your prime years, you will have the chance to put all of your time and energy into pursuing your own goals. Maybe you focus on your career, visit every baseball park in the continental United States, or just devote your time to your new wife and her kids. It certainly seems like a risk worth taking.

Chapter Three: Screwing Up Co-Parenting

Your children will be devastated if you abandon them. When you reject them, your children feel unworthy of love and attention, and this erodes their self-esteem. They might even believe it is their fault, and they will feel guilty for turning you away. Your children will harbor fears that others will abandon them as well, so they grow to distrust people and have difficulty forming tight bonds throughout their lives. Even if your children do welcome you back into their lives after a long absence, they will never forget the pain that you caused by abandoning them, and they will carry their pain and anger into adulthood.

It is also devastating to your children to be minimally involved in their lives. When you fail to attend your children's extracurricular activities, school events, and celebrations, they feel ignored. And when you arrive late for a pickup, return your children early, or substitute a phone call or text for an actual visit, your children feel unimportant to you and unworthy of your time. Your children will learn not to trust anyone, especially you, when you cancel your visits last minute or choose not to show up at all.

Your children will also be sad and disappointed when you do not follow through on the promises you make to them. Even worse, they learn to tolerate disappointment and callous behavior and will come to accept this type of misdeed in future relationships. When their boyfriends or girlfriends fail to show up for a date, instead of getting upset or demanding to be treated appropriately, your children will think of it as normal and acceptable behavior.

- How To Screw Up Your Children -

- Show up late to pick up your children for visitation or drop them off early.

(Your children will feel they are not very important to you.)

- Limit your relationship with your children to infrequent, brief phone calls.

(Your children will feel rejected and will feel undeserving of their parent's love and attention.)

- Make promises to your children and then break them.

(Your children will learn not to trust people, particularly someone they are close to.)

Sabotage Co-Parenting Counseling

Co-parenting is nouveau lingo used to define two people who share the responsibilities of raising the same children even though they are not together. We used to just call it, *divorced parents raising kids.* Some courts now mandate co-parenting counseling where some quack teaches you and your ex how to "communicate effectively" and helps you "develop policies and procedures to govern the children." This is crazy. No one can tell you how to raise your kids! And why would you want to build a co-parenting relationship with your ex-spouse? If having a relationship with your ex worked, you wouldn't be divorced in the first place. The whole thing is ridiculous.

Sure, you are supposed to use this time to clear the lines of communication and focus on issues concerning your children, but you finally have your ex's attention so now is the time to rant about the divorce. Spend the counseling session rehashing old conflicts, fighting about the marriage, examining your breakup, discussing personal issues, and questioning your ex about his life. Discuss anything but the matters at hand, how to best raise your children.

Chapter Three: Screwing Up Co-Parenting

Even if you aren't up for an all out battle with your ex, you could still sabotage co-parent counseling. It's pretty simple; just choose not to commit to the therapy. Don't show up regularly to scheduled appointments, and when you do show up, do not be an active participant. Just sit on the couch and occasionally check your emails on your phone. Do not listen, do not speak openly and honestly, do not share your concerns about your children, do not provide any feedback. However, you must learn the language of co-parenting so both the counselor and your ex will think you are cooperating. Every once in a while say, "We need to work together for the benefit of our kids," or, "Our children need to see us as a united front." Say it with deep conviction, and try not to laugh when the words are coming out of our mouth. Then go back to your emails and texts.

Your calculating ex will probably try to manipulate the counselor so you must be proactive, turn the therapist against your ex, and have he or she align with you. Learn therapist speak and say things that will make your counselor sympathize with your version of events. Turn to your ex and calmly state, "I really felt unappreciated when you didn't thank me for taking the children to the doctor while you were away." The counselor will think your ex is unappreciative, and that you are taken for granted. Also try, "My truth, as I experienced it, is that it was my weekend with the children." The counselor will find you to be patient, kind, and stable under pressure. The more psychobabble you use, the better. Your counselor will believe you are the parent who best understands the co-parenting work and they will be eating out of the palm of your hand. "If our co-parenting relationship wasn't so dysfunctional, and we had more authenticity between us, we could empower our children and help them move on toward a resolution and, ultimately, closure." Score – You 1 : Your Ex 0.

During these sessions, your counselor may teach you the best way to engage with your ex or your children and might dictate parenting rules that you should follow. Do not honor this advice;

just do whatever you want to do instead. However, do not make it obvious that you are intentionally ignoring the counselor's directives. As far as everyone knows, you simply misunderstood. Oops!

Co-parenting counseling and parent coordination can help divorced parents learn to effectively parent together. When these sessions are successful, parents learn to communicate better with one another, address and resolve childcare issues, and obtain day-to-day parenting advice. As a result, there is less parental conflict and less triangulation of the children into their parents' disagreements. This enables smoother transitions, reduces tension when both parents attend their children's activities and events, and, ultimately, decreases the stress in children's everyday lives. When two divorced parents co-parent harmoniously, their children gain the benefit of being parented by a unified force and they feel safer and more secure.

It is important to embrace and commit to co-parenting counseling for the sake of your children. If you are unable to let go of your anger

Chapter Three: Screwing Up Co-Parenting

and resentment over the divorce, or check your emotions at the door, open communication between you and your ex is not possible. If you do not participate actively in these counseling sessions by being honest, providing feedback, and honoring the role of the counselor as a neutral party, they will not be productive. Finally, you must implement the advice of the counselor to enact change and improve the lives of your children.

- How To Screw Up Your Children -

- Use your time in co-parenting counseling to rehash old fights with your ex.

(You will not clear the lines of communication to be able to effectively discuss childcare issues.)

- Use psychobabble to manipulate the co-parenting counselor.

(Without clearly understanding the family dynamics, the co-parenting counselor can not help you and your ex settle disputes or make informed decisions in the best interest of your children.)

- Do not implement any of the directives from the co-parenting counselor.

(Your children will not realize the benefits of the professional advice, and their lives will not improve.)

Screw Up Your Children's Milestones

Life is measured by moments. We watch our children take their first steps, say their first words, and head off to school for their first day of kindergarten. Such simple pleasures. However, as your kids grow up, their milestones become a little more complicated. These events are now perfect opportunities to escalate the conflict with your ex and leave your children with many painful memories.

There are rites of passage, like Bar and Bat Mitzvahs, Baptisms, Holy Communions, Sweet 16s, and Debutante Balls, that offer you the opportunity to screw up your children. Start creating stress in the planning stages. If you are in charge of logistics, do not incorporate your ex's input. If he wants the party on a Saturday, plan it for a Sunday, and if he wants an evening affair, make a brunch. If he hopes to keep the party small and intimate, invite everyone that you know, and then seat his family in the back corner near the bathroom since there is no room near the dance floor. In terms of money, go over budget. Way over! You can't impress your guests without a large band or chateaubriand. When your ex-husband objects to your spending, tell your children that their father does not love them enough to throw them a really great party, so mediocrity will have to do.

The religious milestones are also a great opportunity to argue with your ex over devout beliefs. For example, if you are Jewish, and your son is preparing for his Bar Mitzvah, argue over the type of synagogue you children will attend. If your ex-husband wants a conservative synagogue, choose a reform one. And when your children do not wish to go to the religious school when they are with you, be permissive and let them miss class.

High school graduation is another of your children's achievements that you could easily destroy. The tickets to the commencement might be limited. Make sure to scoop up an extra

Chapter Three: Screwing Up Co-Parenting

ticket for your new boyfriend so that your ex's parents can not both attend. Your children's grandparents did not stay up doing homework with them; you did, and so the ticket is yours. Come graduation day, refuse to sit near your ex and demand your other children sit with you. Give him dirty looks from across the stands, and make it obvious to everyone around that you can not stand him. Let him overhear you congratulate your children, "Lucky you got your brains from me or you might not have made it this far." Plan competing celebrations to mark the happy occasion, and let your children choose which party they will attend.

Screwing up your children can continue even after they become adults. One day they will meet someone, fall in love, and announce that they are getting married. Your children's weddings will be one of the most important milestones in their life, and it also offers endless opportunities to create conflict. Begin from the moment you receive the call from your daughter announcing her engagement. Instead of being excited for her, let her know she's making a big mistake. "You're getting married? That's great news if you are trying to ruin your life." When she reassures you that she has found her soul mate, remind her that you felt the same when you got engaged to her father. Insist that your ex's new wife is left off the invitation. In fact, insist she's left out of the whole affair and threaten not to attend if she is invited.

You are the mother-of-the-bride, and on your daughter's wedding day, everyone must accommodate your needs. Moments before the procession cause a scene and refuse to walk your daughter down the aisle with her father. Then rearrange the whole wedding party so you could be as far away from your ex as possible, and rework the seating, so he isn't anywhere near you for the ceremony. He is lucky you are allowing him to be involved in the wedding at all.

If your ex's new wife does show up against your wishes, make her wish that she hadn't. You hate this woman, and she is not going to ruin your big day. Tell everyone how upset you are, hole yourself up in the ladies' room, and insist your daughter leave the dance floor and come to console you. This is not how you wanted things to go on your special day. When the time comes for your toast, use this moment to remind all of the guests that you did all of the work in raising your beautiful daughter. Raise your glass and say, "I was always there to care for you when you were sick, to hold your hand after your many breakups, and to console you when your father wasn't giving you any attention, and I'm so happy to share this day with you." Don't bother to mention the groom. One day in the future, he'll be ancient history.

The birth of your first grandchild will be one of the most exciting days of your life. You should be at the hospital with your children eagerly awaiting the news, and your ex-husband should be nowhere in sight. You can not stand being in the same room as him, and you do not want him to ruin your special day. Once the baby is born, insist the little angel be named for someone on your side of the family. You are making a difficult task easier by narrowing down the options. If the child is named for anyone in your ex's family, refuse to call the child by the proper name, and just refer to him or her as "the baby."

* * *

CHAPTER THREE: SCREWING UP CO-PARENTING

If you hold onto to unresolved anger and resentment from your divorce, your negative feeling can ruin your children's happy occasions from their elementary school years into adulthood. They will be anxious in anticipation of a conflict between their parents before their graduations, weddings, and even the birth of their own children. The events themselves will be stressful and exhausting for them rather than joyful and exhilarating as they try to manage your anger, and they will be humiliated if you lash out in public. Your children are placed in the middle of your conflict when they must try to satisfy all of your demands, their other parent's needs, and their desires for these special events. Your children deserve to have their milestones witnessed, supported, and celebrated by both of their parents. It's important to put your love for your children ahead of your hatred for your ex, especially at these times.

- How To Screw Up Your Children -

- Create stress around the planning of your children's milestones.

(Your children will dread special occasions, rather than look forward to them.)

- Cause conflict with your ex at your children's graduations.

(Your children will feel frustrated and hurt that you can not put aside your feelings and celebrate their important events with their other parent.)

- Make excessive demands during your children's weddings.

(When your needs are at odds with your children's desires for their wedding, trying to appease you will cause them stress and grief, and you will ruin the memory of their special day forever.)

Dive Into A New Relationship

Before the ink dries on your divorce papers, you should be out hunting for a new partner. If you move quickly into a new relationship, you will never be lonely, you will feel loved, and could share the burden of raising your children with someone else. Just to add some icing to the cake, imagine how jealous your ex will be when he finds out you are in a relationship with Mr. Handsome N. Successful?

It's a game of numbers so you should become a serial dater, and make sure to introduce your children to all of your casual new prospects. Have every Tom, Dick and Harry all move in and out of your children's lives with close succession. When you finally think you have met someone with a little-staying power, introduce him to the kids not as a "friend" or by his first name. Tell them, "This is going to be your new daddy." He is your soul mate, the real deal, and you are certain of this after the first few dates. This guy is the total package and a huge upgrade from your children's father, who it turns out, was just a big mistake. In the

Chapter Three: Screwing Up Co-Parenting

excitement of it all, don't bother to discuss anything serious, like your future together or even his feelings about having children.

Rather than ease your new lover into the family, integrate him into your lives immediately. Have him start staying overnight right away so he can spend a lot of time getting to know the kids. In fact, have him at your home all of the time and include him in all of your activities. You are one big happy family, so there is no need to carve out any time to spend with your kids alone. If you want him around, the kids must want him around too. And, while he's hanging out with your children, speak to him openly about your ex-husband. Talk about all the ways your children's father is flawed and compliment him on everything that he does better.

You and your new boyfriend should show the world how much you love each other. When you are around your children, whether at home relaxing on the couch or sitting in the bleachers at your son's football game, you should snuggle up together like two teenagers experiencing first love. Do not hold back the physical affection. If your kids let on that all of the hanky-panky makes them uncomfortable, be dismissive and tell them they are just jealous that they don't have anyone to love.

Should your children get out of line, give your new boyfriend the authority to discipline them. Let him put them in time out, take away their cell phones, and send them to bed without dinner. This will let your kids know he is a boss. If your children protest, which they will, tell them their father never taught them to respect their elders.

***

Divorce: The Art of Screwing Up Your Children

You might find it difficult to be alone after your divorce. However, if you start dating soon after your marital separation or divorce, it can be very hard on your children. Your children need time to adjust and heal after the breakup of their family, and they may still be struggling with their feelings about the divorce even if you have moved on. There are, however, ways to make it easier on them. Do not introduce your children to every person whom you date casually, because the procession of people rotating in and out of their lives will threaten their stability. Only introduce your children to someone you are seeing once the relationship becomes serious. Take time to get to know your partner and make sure that you are on the same page about your future, especially when it comes to children. Your children may grow attached to your new partner, and if you later realize you disagree on important issues and the relationship ends, your children will also experience the loss. Finally, never compare your ex to your new partner in a demeaning way. This is just another form of badmouthing.

Remember, your children might feel threatened by your relationship and the time and attention you are devoting to your new partner. If

Chapter Three: Screwing Up Co-Parenting

you neglect your children, they will get angry and will begin to hate the person who is taking you away from them. *Your children may protest at first, but after being ignored continually, they will give up and just accept that you are unavailable to them. So make sure to take things slow. At the beginning of the relationship, do not have your new partner stay overnight when you have your children, do not involve him or her in every family activity, and make sure to schedule one-on-one time for you and your children.*

Children of divorce complain about two things that they find most annoying about their parent's new relationships. First, they are disturbed by excessive displays of affection between their parent and his or her new partner. Whether it is in public or in private, children are embarrassed by this behavior, and they are especially uncomfortable when they hardly know the love interest. Your children model themselves after you, and this conduct also gives them the green light to get physical with people before they get to know them well, and this may lower their barriers to promiscuity. Children's other pet peeve is being disciplined by a parent's boyfriend or girlfriend. Your children will resent your partner acting with unearned and premature parental authority, and they will be angry with you for letting it happen.

- How To Screw Up Your Children -

- Quickly introduce your children to your new girlfriends or boyfriends.

(Your children might become attached to these people, and if the relationships do not work out, they will experience losses in addition to the breakup of the family.)

- Display excessive physical affection in public.

(Your public displays of affection will embarrass and humiliate your children.)

- Allow your new partner to discipline your children.

(Your children will resent your new partner exerting parental authority over them and will become angry with both of you.)

Batter Your Ex's Boyfriend

Occasionally, a display of brute force is warranted and necessary. Words are lovely, but physical aggression gets right to the point. Remember this the next time you have a confrontation with your ex-wife's rebound. If he moves in on your family too quickly or disrespects you, just throw a punch. That will teach him! Make sure the fight occurs before a captive audience, including your children, so everyone knows how much tougher and stronger you are than him.

Violence is inexcusable. Not only will you frighten your children, but also modeling this behavior teaches them to combat hurt feelings and resolve conflicts using physical force. You are also showing them it is acceptable to assault their spouse or marry someone who is abusive.

- How To Screw Up Your Children -

- Get into physical fights with your ex's new partner.

(Your children will learn to use physical aggression to resolve conflict.)

Start A Family Feud

Your ex is the enemy, and by extension, so is his entire family. This is true regardless of what your relationship was before the divorce. Your sister-in-law might have been your closest friend. Not anymore. She is one of them, and you can no longer trust her. Treat her with the coldness and disrespect she deserves. Snub your in-laws at family gatherings, ignore their phone calls and texts, and trash them to anyone who will listen. This is war.

You must turn your children against your ex's family so that they align with your side of the battle. Even if your children have a history of warm, loving relationships with these relatives, it is not too late. They are horrible people, and they have betrayed you. Criticize their character and question their judgment so that your children lose respect for them. Spill their family secrets, like the alcoholic grandmother or the promiscuous aunt. Share all of the questionable things you learned about them throughout your years of marriage. If you still have not succeeded in turning your children against their other parent's family, restrict access between your ex's family and your kids.

Don't go into battle alone. Escalate the conflict until everyone is involved, and create tribal warfare between the two families. It is pretty simple. Just mention all of the things your ex's family has said about your family in confidence and vice versa. Take the text out of context, distort it, or, if you must, make stuff up. Just continue to aggravate the situation until everyone is up in arms.

Your children deserve to maintain a healthy relationship with all of their relatives. They most likely think of both sides of their extended family as a source of emotional support and love, and they surrender these gifts when you turn them against one side of their family. When you spill your ex's family secrets or celebrate their misdeeds, your children lose respect for the same people that they are supposed to turn to for guidance. Additionally, treating your ex's family disrespectfully teaches your children that it is acceptable to act callously towards others. This kind of behavior negatively affects your children into their future by teaching them to be disrespect toward family relationships.

When your children's two families are at war, they are stuck in the middle of a large-scale conflict. There is palpable tension surrounding every celebrated milestone and family gathering, and these events are sources of great stress for your children. To minimize this conflict, they may lie to protect themselves or in extreme cases, sever ties from one side of the family.

- How To Screw Up Your Children -

- Treat your ex's family with disrespect and disdain.

(This will teach your children that it is acceptable to be disrespectful to your spouse's family.)

- Reveal your ex's family secrets to your children.

(Your children will lose respect for their loved ones, and they will feel ashamed to be part of their family.)

- Instigate fights between the two families by divulging the things they've said to you in confidence about each other.

(Family events will be filled with tension and anxiety.)

Litigate Over And Over Again

Your original divorce trial was just a jumping off point to begin a lifetime of litigation with your ex. Litigate as often as legally possible. It is an excellent way to get back at your ex and to mess with your children.

If your ex does not follow every word of the settlement, do not bother discussing it with her, file a contempt suit. When you decide on a whim, you would like to change the custody agreement, file a modification action and drag her into court. And when she is bothering you, request a restraining order. That will teach her not to mess with you. You should consult with your attorney about how frequently to file contempt suits. Filing too many in a short period may be considered harassment, but not filing often enough can prove ineffective. In this case, do whatever your shark recommends. A contempt action is also an excellent way to justify a modification suit. First, imply that your ex-spouse did not follow the parenting plan. That is the contempt portion. Next, request that the parenting plan be changed to restrict her access to the children and give you more power and control.

Litigation is costly and time-consuming, and, therefore, it is the best way to exact your revenge. Bury your ex-wife with discovery requests, demand an absurd amount of documentation, subject her to depositions, hearings, and trials, and force her to spend every cent of her retirement savings paying lawyers to defend her case. If she makes more money than you, rub salt in the wound and request that she pay for your legal fees.

Your children will certainly appreciate the legal drama as well. Imagine how boring your kids' lives would be if everyone just got along and life was calm and predictable. As a bonus, they will get a break from their parents' focus and attention since you will both be too busy and preoccupied litigating your disagreements to be concerned about them. It's the parenting that most kids dream about, and it will certainly help to screw them up.

The goal of all of the legal actions should be to restrict your ex's access to the children. Restricting access increases your power and authority over your kids and your ex. Ask for the moon and the stars, and the judge will usually grant you at least a couple constellations.

CHAPTER THREE: SCREWING UP CO-PARENTING

When you continue to bring your ex to court to resolve co-parenting issues after your divorce, you are unfair to your children. They are dragged back into the middle of their parents' conflict, and they have to re-experience the same negative thoughts and feelings that they did during the original divorce litigation. With repeat litigation, the children re-experience this stress over and over again. These ongoing lawsuits cause your children to lose hope that the feud will eventually end, and they feel doomed to a life where their parents will always be at war. Additionally, your children will model your behavior learning to be unforgiving and vindictive, and they will turn to the court system to resolve their personal disputes in the future.

- How To Screw Up Your Children -

- File many contempt and modification lawsuits.

(This will expose your children to perpetual levels of high conflict and will leave them feeling hopeless that there will ever be peace. It also teaches your children that personal differences should be resolved in courts.)

- Allege that your children can not handle the current parenting schedule and that you need to be granted sole physical and legal custody.

(Your children will be frustrated that their lives continue to be disrupted by being put in the middle of their parents' fights.)

Alienate The Other Parent

You hate your ex, and you want your children to hate her too. You wish that she would just go away and that you could be the only parent in your children's lives. Unfortunately, she is a good mother, your children still want her around, and the courts have done nothing to stop her. Do you have any other options? Yes! You must turn your children against your ex using any means at your disposal. If you have come this far in the book, you have already learned much of what you need to know.

First things first, make sure your children feel more attached to you and like you are better than your ex. Spoil them rotten. Use all of the economic resources you can access to marginalize your ex-wife and gain favor with your children, and then constantly remind your children of just how generous you are. Be the more lenient parent, the fun one that relaxes the rules and allows them to get away with everything. Encourage their co-dependence by telling your children how much you love them and need them. You have made many sacrifices for them through the years, and they owe you one.

You must convince your children that their mother is evil. Remember to use badmouthing and triangulation techniques that are guaranteed to work. Place the blame on her for everything that has been wrong in the marriage and hold her responsible for

Chapter Three: Screwing Up Co-Parenting

the divorce. Point out her mistakes and criticize her parenting in front of your children. Even if you know she is a great mother; the idea is to alter your children's perception. Engaging in these behaviors will cause your children to lose respect for her. If your children ever voice a minor complaint against her, like she made them do chores, agree with them and then blow it way out of proportion. You want your ex to look like the bad parent and you the good parent. You need your children to see you as the only parent capable of providing comfort and guidance.

Now that you have laid the groundwork, it is time to let your children choose. Who do they want to be with? Set up temptations that coincide with their mother's parenting time and force your children to pick what they would rather do. Encourage them to decide whether or not they want to visit with their mother. Hopefully, they pick you, and they refuse to see her.

If you have not convinced your children to distance themselves from their mother, you must make your children feel that she is uninterested. Withhold all information that you can about your children so that their mother can not be involved in their everyday lives. Do not share the dates of your children's school plays or dance recitals, and if she sends you emails asking for information, delay your response until it is too late for her to attend. This way she looks like a no-show, and your children assume she was just too busy for them. Do not include your ex on making important decisions about medical care or education.

You should also employ tactics you have learned thus far to restrict your ex's access to the children. Rigidly stick to the parenting schedule, be inflexible, and overschedule the children with extra-curricular activities during their mother's parenting time. When she calls to talk to the children, tell her they are busy studying or out with friends. Of course, if you never pass along the messages, your children will start to think that their mother does not care to speak with them. You should also limit contact with her family and her friends. Your children do not need those people in their lives. If you want to make her a ghost, get rid of pictures with your ex and change your children's last name so they will not feel tied to her in any way.

As a last resort, you should start to give your children the impression that their mother is dangerous. Highlight all of the times she lost her cool and got angry with them. Maybe she raised her voice a little or doled out a deserved punishment, but convince your children that what they experienced was terror and that they fear for their safety when they are with her. That will also explain to everyone out there why you have limited their mother's access to the children. Since she is abusive and unsafe to be around, ask for supervised visitation. Then she will not enjoy any alone time with the children, and their relationship is bound to suffer.

Parental alienation is the process through which one parent turns the children against their other parent by manipulating them into disrespecting, fearing, or hating that parent. Much like brainwashing,

Chapter Three: Screwing Up Co-Parenting

the alienating parent distorts their children's perception of the targeted parent. The children begin to doubt their own experiences of their other parent and adopt the same thoughts and feelings of the parent that is alienating them. Eventually, the children lose awareness of how they initially felt about their alienated parent. This interference in the children's relationship with their other parent destroys the attachment bond those children have to that parent.

Parental Alienation explains why some children of divorce are hesitant or refuse to visit with one of their parents when the parent is neither abusive nor neglectful. In severe cases of alienation, the children will completely cut off contact with the targeted parent, refusing even minimal interaction. It is not uncommon in these serious cases of alienation for a child to express hatred and disdain for the same parent they previously loved and admired.

Restrictive Gatekeeping is one dynamic leading to parental alienation. One parent controls information about and access to the children. This is not done for safety. It is done to control the children and the other parent. Most restrictive gatekeepers believe they are protective gatekeepers just looking to keep their children safe. They are not aware that their behaviors are contributing to the unhealthy estrangement between their children and their other parent.

Destroying your children's relationship with their other parent is a form of psychological abuse. These children suffer the loss of a capable and loving parent. Often, they also lose their relationship with their extended family and friends. Victims of parental alienation also experience low self-esteem, self-hatred, a lack of trust, higher rates of depression, and a greater risk for substance abuse.

- How To Screw Up Your Children -

- Manipulate your children into refusing to visit with their other parent.

(This form of brainwashing will destroy your children's mental and emotional health.)

- Do all you can to restrict your ex-spouse from regular visits with the children.

(Your children will lose the love and support of a capable parent.)

- Try to convince your children that your ex is abusive.

(Alienating your children from their other parent is itself a form of child abuse.)

Rewrite History

Here's an excellent concept: take any experience from the past and put a whole new spin on the story. It's called *historical revisionism* (psychologists just love fancy words), and what it means is that you can simply change the memory of the past to suit your agenda.

Many screenwriters have used historical revisionism to re-tell a historical event the way they feel it occurred, or should have occurred, regardless if the facts match their storyline or not. This strategy is especially useful when you want your children to remember something, not as it occurred, but as you wish it happened.

Let's give it a try…

Chapter Three: Screwing Up Co-Parenting

"Remember your championship baseball game? Your dad was ~~5 minutes~~ over an hour late because he was ~~up against a difficult work deadline~~ grabbing a beer with his buddies. He missed ~~nothing except the singing of the national anthem~~ your triple to left field, and you were ~~so happy to see him in the bleachers when you got up to bat~~ devastated he wasn't there to see it. I ~~was so annoyed he made it to the game~~ felt so bad for you. ~~Very few~~ All of the other fathers were there to see their kids' big plays. Your team ~~tied the game~~ got crushed, so I took you ~~home for a bath~~ out for ice cream to help ease the pain. What a terrible night."

This technique can be used to alter trivial days or significant milestones in your children's lives. It is easy to manipulate your children's memories of people, places, and activities, particularly if they were young at the time you were referencing. You can make yourself look like parent-of-the-year and your ex-spouse look like a huge disappointment at past birthday parties, school plays, and graduations or on any given Sunday afternoon. When retelling old stories from your revised perspective, make sure to add an emotional component. It is critical to tell your children not just what they saw, but how they felt about it. This will really screw them up!

It is also quite effective to turn their memories and feelings about the past from positive to negative. "Remember our old house, the one that always had leaks in the basement… Your third-grade production of Annie was really hard to watch. Nobody sang on key… Every time we went to visit your grandparents, you and your brother fought during the whole car ride." If you repeat the negative comments enough, your children will eventually agree with you, and they will start to believe their entire past, including their friends, activities, schools, and the time spent with your ex, was chaotic, horrible, and tumultuous.

Your children might have a different memory than you do. If so, remind them how young they were at the time and how unreliable their memory is. Over time and with repeated storytelling, they will start to remember the event exactly the way you want them to. Voila! You've changed history.

When you reinterpret events from the past so that the story better suits your agenda, you are manipulating your children's understanding of what they experienced, and undermining their reliance on their memory and processing of past events. Your children will stop trusting their own thoughts and feelings and will learn to depend on your interpretation of events. Psychologists refer to the process of changing other's thoughts and memories as memory contamination. You might know this process as brainwashing.

When you take it a step further and replace children's good memories with bad ones, you cause even more damage. Your children now also think that these past events were terrible or traumatic, when they may have actually been good experiences, and once your children's memories are tainted, they will always have this negative view of their past.

- How To Screw Up Your Children -

- Try to change the way your children remember past events.

(Your children will learn to distrust their own thoughts, experiences, and perceptions.)

- Tell your children how they supposedly felt about past events.

(Your children will become less aware of their feelings.)

- Reinterpret happy memories as negative ones.

(Your children will believe their lives were filled with unhappiness.)

Chapter Four: Screwing up the Everyday

Remarry A Monster

When you decide to remarry, do not intend on doing it *Brady-Bunch*-style. Your goal is to screw up your children, and creating a beautifully blended family will not maximize their unhappiness. A dysfunctional stepfamily will create many opportunities to make them miserable.

First, pick an awful guy - a new husband your children will despise. If he has trouble managing his anger, lashes out at others, is unkind, extremely critical, he is perfect for you. Whenever your children criticize your new partner, assume they are jealous or that their father is brainwashing them. It can't be that your children are correct in their assessment of the new love of your life. View the man's fanaticism with cleanliness and organization as character strength rather than as a sign that he is a controlling tyrant who will be critical of anything that is not done his way.

Allow and encourage your new husband to discipline your children. This could be a bonding experience. Make your children call your new husband "dad." Have them refer to their father by his first name. When they protest, demand this as a show of respect, even though you are doing it only to hurt your ex-husband.

Chapter Four: Screwing up the Everyday

Move your family into the home of your new husband and demand that your children follow all of his house rules. Make your kids share bedrooms, while your stepchildren continue to have rooms of their own. Don't bring any of your old furniture or personal belongings to the new house. You are starting over and want to shed any of the furnishings that could remind the children of life with their father.

If you become a stepparent, take authority over your stepchildren's lives. Their mother is crazy, according to your new husband; so don't worry about undermining her authority. Scold them, criticize them, and make them perform all of the household chores. If your stepchildren complain about you or your children, punish them with the cold shoulder. Ignoring them is an effective way to send the message that you will not tolerate criticism of you or your children.

Your children, of course, are smarter, prettier, and more special than their stepsiblings and they deserve better. Your stepchildren will understand their place in the home if you maintain a double standard when it comes to following the house rules. Your children can err at times because they have the best intentions, but your stepchildren lose phone privileges for the same infractions.

If your new husband complains that you treat his children differently from your own, tell him his ex-wife must be poisoning the children against you. Let him know you need his support to overcome the evil influence of his ex-wife. It may not satisfy him, but never own up to any double standard.

* * *

Blending a family together takes a long time, not days or weeks. When you remarry, it can be very difficult for your children. Your remarriage ruins their fantasy that their parents will reconcile. Children need time to adjust to the new arrangement and time to get to know their new stepparent. Do not demand they love and accept your new partner; allow the relationship a chance to build. It is also important that your children know they are not replacing their biological parent and that you do not force them to choose between the two.

When it comes to combining different families together, it is important that the biological parent serves as the primary disciplinarian and nurturer. The stepparent only plays a supportive role, especially in the early years of the relationship. Both adults should agree on and set the household rules that all of the children must follow, and they should hold both sets of children to the same standard of behavior. Otherwise, frustration and resentment will build between the stepsiblings.

If you are moving into your new husband or wife's house, your kids will initially feel like strangers in what is supposed to be their home. If there is conflict between the children and a stepparent, or between stepsiblings, the house will no longer be a place of comfort and refuge;

it will be a place in which your children will feel awkward, scrutinized, disapproved of, and ultimately unwelcome. Your kids are likely to make excuses to stay away from your house.

- How To Screw Up Your Children -

- Remarry a person your children dislike.

(Your children will believe that their feelings are not important to you.)

- Discipline your stepchildren more harshly than your own children.

(Your behavior towards your stepchildren will breed resentment between the stjpgiblings and rage toward you.)

Air Your Grievances Online

Social media can be a great tool to help you cope with your divorce. You should become an active user, and create a large online network. I'm sure you have already linked to your friends, but it's time to build a massive following by adding acquaintances, colleagues, and people you meet in Starbucks while waiting for your latte. Now you have a huge platform to publicize your complaints, and a community of people willing to rage against your injustices.

More importantly, you must *friend* your children on Facebook (you should also track them on Twitter and follow them on Instagram). Why stop there? Also, connect with their friends and their friends' friends. It will appear that you are just a responsible parent monitoring your children's online activity, but now your children and their friends have access to your status, complaints, and observations and, of course, the comments that these posts receive.

You should publish stories about all the miserable things your ex has done in the past, and add to your timeline all the things that he does in real time. This way all of your Facebook friends, including your children, will get to know what a no-good loser he is. Hopefully, users will comment on what they see, and your children can read the public consensus on their father as seen by your loyalists.

Here is a sample social media post with responses from friends:

> **NewlyDivorced:** The ex did it again. #whatanidiot. #latewithkids.
>
> **FriendForever:** Prolly at his GF doing u no what. What a sleazebag.
>
> **IGotYourBack:** Rather sleep with scank than get kids to places on time.
>
> **NewlyDivorced:** You all know what I deal with. #wantkidstounderstand
>
> **I GotYourBack:** #tellthemeverything LOL

Be sure to like Facebook pages titled *Self-Centered Ex-Spouse* and *Divorce that Loser*, join groups called *I Hate My Ex*, and share articles about bad parenting, child abuse allegations, and corrupt family courts that always side with fathers. It is a subtle, yet effective way of sending messages to your children.

Don't forget to brag to your social network how brave your children are for dealing with your awful ex and how much they have

CHAPTER FOUR: SCREWING UP THE EVERYDAY

overcome as the children of divorce. Include their names and photos and tag them in the posts so there is no question about their identity. If your children ask you to remove your public postings, just ignore them and continue divulging their private information. Now all of their friends, relatives, and acquaintances know all of the delicate details of their lives, and this will add considerably to your children's distress. That is your goal, isn't it?

Broadcasting negative information about you and your family on the Internet might help relieve your pain, but it hurts your children. They will feel embarrassed, humiliated, and ashamed when their private business becomes the source of public ridicule. They will be upset if their parent has been criticized before such a wide audience, but, ultimately, they will be angry with you for revealing the information.

Sending subtle messages to your children via online postings, rather than talking to them candidly about the issues surrounding your divorce, will teach them that verbal, direct communication is needless. They too will resort to uploading passive-aggressive diatribes instead of speaking openly and honestly to others about their feelings.

- How To Screw Up Your Children -

- Friend your children on social media.

(*This will allow your children access to your social media posts, many of which are critical of your children's other parent.*)

- Leave hostile comments and negative allegations about your ex on social media.

(*Your children will feel angry that you are publicly ridiculing their other parent.*)

- Post personal stories about your children and how they are dealing with the divorce.

(*Your children will be embarrassed by the exposure of their personal information to such a wide, public audience.*)

Dress For Success

It's time to dress to impress. You are young, wild, and free, and you'll want to choose the attire that best projects this new image. Remember, you never get a second chance to make a first impression, and you are looking for some action.

If you are a woman, dress like a Kardashian. Think short dresses, plunging necklines, and sky-high stilettos. Make time to get eyelash extensions and a few rounds of Botox, and if you aren't afraid to go under the knife, *accentuate the positive* a cup size or two. The bigger, the better. If your teenagers protest, don't worry. They just wish they could look as hot as you do.

Chapter Four: Screwing up the Everyday

You know you are dressing appropriately if your children's male friends flirt with you. They will think you are the hottest mom on the block, and you are sure to get all of the male attention you've been craving. The other women in the neighborhood will shake their heads in disgust. But who cares? They are mostly unhappy, dull housewives who secretly crave the excitement you now have.

If you are a man, get a tattoo. Open an extra button on your shirt and pop your collar the way that Justin Bieber does. You are not some old guy whining over politics and worrying about his stock portfolio. You listen to Jay Z while killin' it in your new Corvette — #winning. You are cool and relevant, and one day your children will appreciate how awesome you are.

Children are very aware of their parents' behavior, including how they dress. If you dress age-inappropriately, you will embarrass your children, especially your teenagers. They find this behavior disturbing, and they will try to distance themselves from you. Children feel the same way when their parents start to act younger than they are and begin to behave like their peers instead of their protectors. Children need consistency while coping with your divorce, and any obvious deviation in your behavior can trigger intense anxiety for them.

- How To Screw Up Your Children -

- Dress like a teenager.

(Your children will feel anxious seeing a change in your behavior.)

- Go out in public with your children while decked out in your new, age-inappropriate attire.

(Your children will be embarrassed and feel ashamed to have a parent like you.)

Don't Worry About Child Development

There is no need to protect your children. They are not fragile. One day before you know it, they will be adults, so they must start preparing now.

If you would like to help your children grow up quickly, pile on adult responsibilities. Why should they be out riding bikes or socializing with friends while you do all the work? In addition to making the beds, emptying the dishwasher, and taking out the trash, have them maintain the yard and cook dinner for the family. You could sit back, relax, watch TV, and enjoy some "me" time while they are attending to their chores. Tell your son he is the man of the house. It is his obligation to protect the family and keep everyone safe. Tell your daughter she is in charge of taking care of her younger siblings and helping you through the divorce. Maybe your children lose out on a carefree childhood? Big deal. Plenty of people have an awful childhood and survive.

CHAPTER FOUR: SCREWING UP THE EVERYDAY

In fact, since you are treating your children with such maturity, you can tell them all of the details about your divorce from their father. They are old enough to hear it, and even if they are not, they will be some day. Share with them the ugly truth about their other parent, even if it concerns adult issues. While you are at it, tell your kids that Santa Claus does not exist, and the Easter Bunny is a hoax conjured up to sell candy. Prince Charming? He ended up leaving Cinderella for one of her ugly stepsisters.

Children need adult leadership to feel safe and secure. Without it, they do not have a sense of limits and may feel that things going on around them, or even their own behavior, may spin out of control. When

children lack limits and direction and are treated at a developmental stage they have not yet attained, their anxiety increases.

Telling your son he is the man of the house will burden him. Children need to feel that adults are in charge and protecting them from harm. Giving a child the idea that they must protect the family can overwhelm them, leaving them feeling stressed by the responsibility to care for siblings and even a parent. Letting a child know they are responsible for caring for their siblings also saddles that child with responsibilities that are not age appropriate. The result is increased anxiety and possible a desire to escape the situation. Burdening your children with too much responsibility will likely result in them growing up to either take on too much responsibility for others or become careless and irresponsible.

You must also be careful about what you disclose to your children about your divorce. If you reveal more than what is appropriate for their age or their mental and emotional development, they will be confused and overwhelmed. They are likely to misunderstand the allegations they hear or misinterpret the information they are given.

- How To Screw Up Your Children -

- Delegate adult responsibilities to your children, including caring for their younger siblings.

(Your children will feel burdened and anxious.)

- Do not consider the age of your children when sharing information with them about your divorce.

(Your children might misconstrue information they can not understand.)

Drown Your Sorrows

Who doesn't enjoy a cold beer at the end of a long day? A bottle of Amstel, a glass of champagne, Maker's Mark on the rocks, or a spicy margarita - whatever your drink of choice may be, you know how to handle your liquor, so the more the merrier. You are going through a rough patch, and this is not the time to limit yourself. Here's an even better idea: Add prescription pills or marijuana to the mix, and the hearty cocktail of booze and drugs will help you block out the pain of your divorce and deal with the strains of single parenthood.

You don't need to be present anyway. Your children could fend for themselves. They can hitch rides to and from soccer practice, prepare their own dinners, and tell themselves when it's time to shut off the television and go to bed.

Your teens will especially love caring for a dependent parent. Rather than socialize with friends, study for exams, or cultivate their interests, they will get to spend all of their free time picking up for your slack. Rather than thinking about taking care of themselves, they will expend all of their energy worrying about you.

You should refuse to control your problem. (What problem)? Refuse to get help. Refuse even to discuss the issue with your children. You could stop whenever YOU want to stop. Let your children know if it weren't for your ex, you wouldn't need to drink at all. You can't handle all of this stress sober, and if they continue to nag you, you'll certainly never change. Tell them to never again mention the subject of your drinking.

* * *

Divorce: The Art of Screwing Up Your Children

Parents' drug or alcohol abuse creates an extremely dangerous environment for their children. Being intoxicated severely compromises a parent's ability to make healthy and safe parenting decisions. The result is that their children are more likely to face hazardous situations. The impaired parent may take the children for a car ride or leave them home unsupervised, without appreciating the risk. An intoxicated parent is unable to think clearly and rationally, and therefore, also ill-equipped to handle emergencies.

Children do not understand addiction, and they are very disturbed by their parent's inability to stop a dangerous, destructive, and possibly illegal behavior. They may feel responsible for their parent's drinking or drug use, or at least to blame for not stopping it. Furthermore, children constantly worry that something bad will happen to the addicted parent. This guilt, fear, and anxiety may impact many areas of the children's life.

When addicted parents refuse to acknowledge or discuss their problems with their children or try to cover them up, the lines of communication close down. Children learn that it is better to ignore uncomfortable subjects than discuss them openly. *Parents who abuse alcohol and drugs place their children at higher risk for using and abusing alcohol and drugs or getting into relationships with people who have addictions.*

- How To Screw Up Your Children -

- Drink and use drugs in excess.

(This will make it impossible for you to care properly for your children.)

- Blame your substance abuse on your ex-spouse.

(Your children will learn to blame their own inappropriate behaviors or problems on other people.)

- Refuse to speak to your children about their concerns over your alcohol or drug use.

(You will close the lines of communication between you and your children.)

Proclaim Your Moral Superiority

Proclaim your moral superiority to your children, friends, family, and ex-husband. Remind everyone that you are an upstanding citizen and a "good (Christian, Jew, Muslim, etc.)." Professing your moral superiority gives you immediate credibility. How can a religious person ever do anything harmful to their children? After all, it is like a seal of approval for wholesomeness, virtue, morality, and just plain doing the right thing.

Couch all your parenting decisions in religious terms. Quote your favorite scriptures liberally, and use those quotes to justify what you want and any behavior you engage in. If you are heavy on discipline, remind your children that sparing the rod will spoil them. Who would argue your right to expose your children to your religious teachings? If you search the scriptures enough, you will find passages to justify any of your behaviors, including murder, theft, multiple sexual partners, animal sacrifice, and having children out of wedlock. It's all about finding the right passages and proper editing, even if you have to take some things entirely out of context.

There are moral and religious aspects to many decisions you make in your children's life. By justifying your beliefs and actions in moral terms, you give an air of superiority and wisdom to your decisions and behavior. It doesn't matter if you use your morality to engage in prejudice or discrimination, as long as it sounds moral and like the right thing to do.

If someone, particularly your ex, criticizes your behavior, accuse them of not following your religion's laws. Let your children know their father is a nonbeliever, destined to spend eternity rotting in the bowels of Hell. You know your scripture, and this is a moral and religious fight for the souls of your children. You have to make sure your children escape eternal damnation. Saving your kids is your moral obligation. It is of particular importance to appear morally superior while bashing your ex-husband.

Should you stumble and fall, such as getting pregnant with your new flame out of wedlock when all that PDA gets carried away, don't take responsibility for that inappropriate situation. Turn that negative into a positive. Let your children know the new baby is Heaven-sent and that it was God's will for you to get pregnant. Make sure the children understand that it is not the

Chapter Four: Screwing up the Everyday

same as an irresponsible, promiscuous teenager becoming an unwed mother. God's will can become your best rationale for anything you want to do and your best alibi for anything you've done wrong.

Don't even worry if you are pulled over for a DUI. After all, the devil made you do it. It's highly likely that you were driven to drink by that conniving ex-husband of yours. What a beautiful way out you have for all of your inappropriate behavior. You will never look bad. Your children will always think you are a saint, truly holy, as long as any bad behavior is always the influence of some demonic force.

A religious person like you would never be considered abusive to either your children or your ex-husband. This free pass allows you to be verbally inappropriate to your ex-husband and the children without repercussion. Everyone who knows you will swear you would never say anything inappropriate since you are such a religious person.

When your children point out that there is a discrepancy between your behavior and your religious beliefs, punish them. Don't ever let them think you are a hypocrite. They have no right to question your morals. Explain that this is like doubting the existence of God, something you do not want them ever to do.

* * *

Using religious explanations to justify all of your decisions and behavior can be damaging to your kids. This is particularly true when you are justifying your bad behavior as either the result of God's will or a demonic force. Your children will see the discrepancy between what you teach and the realities of your conduct. They will see you as the hypocrite you are.

Your children will also come to see you as woefully out of touch with the consequences of your decisions and behavior. They will begin to understand that you lack insight into your actions. Hopefully, they will not model their behavior after you.

CHAPTER FOUR: SCREWING UP THE EVERYDAY

- How To Screw Up Your Children -

- Proclaim your moral superiority to your children and your ex-spouse.

(This will teach your children about arrogance.)

- Justify all your behavior by saying you are following the dictates of your religion.

(Your children will feel you try to justify everything you do, regardless if it is really a moral issue or just your personal preference.)

- Don't worry about your behavior not being consistent with your moral teachings.

(Your children will learn that you are a hypocrite.)

Protect Your Kids From All Of The World's Dangers

Your ex-husband always accuses you of being too easy on your children, and he criticizes you for being an overprotective parent. You are not overprotective and definitely not controlling! You love your children, and you just want to shield them from the physical and emotional dangers that surround them. Without him at home, you are now free to raise your children the way you want. You can keep them calm, comfortable, and safe all of the time.

You might not be able to cover your kids in bubble wrap without looking crazy, but you can certainly forbid them from doing anything that poses a modicum of risk. Refuse to let your preteens leave the house alone, ride bikes around the neighborhood, or cross the street without adult supervision. You've seen the news; danger lurks behind every corner. When you are anxious that your children will be staying with their other parent, give them each a cell phone, and tell them to call you when they are afraid. You are pretty certain their father's house is a very scary place. And since you can not trust that other parents are capable of watching your kids, do not allow your teenagers to attend sleepovers or birthday parties where you can not monitor their every move. You are only looking out for your children's best interest. Football and baseball are definite no-nos. They could get hit in the head with the ball and get a concussion. Then what? In fact, there will be no organized sports at all. And finally, and most importantly, DO NOT LET YOUR TEENAGERS DATE! Dating will only lead to heartbreak, and you can not stand to see your children upset.

You must also protect your children from all of the food allergies and environmental toxins that threaten their health. Even if several pediatricians have ruled conclusively that your children are not at risk, you can never be too cautious. No gluten. No flour. No dairy. No sugar. Birthday cake is not an exception! Your blacklist also includes inorganic vegetables, tap water, and anything with food coloring. Since you can not risk your children ingesting any of these accidently, make sure their school does not allow any outside food to be served. Demand that the school stops using cleaning products in your children's classrooms. Detoxify your home by tearing up all of the carpeting and getting rid of all synthetic fabrics and plastics that can slowly contaminate your children. You must also refuse to get your children vaccinated. Why risk all of the harmful side effects that you have read about online? These poisons are simply a way for drug manufacturers to make money. Be a constant reminder to your children that all of these substances can easily make them sick.

CHAPTER FOUR: SCREWING UP THE EVERYDAY

If you want your children to be happy all of the time, you should also allow them to avoid all of the things that make them uncomfortable. If they refuse to go to school, indulge them. If they are too anxious to go on play-dates, let them stay home. And if they do not like the dentist, cancel their appointments. Heck, even you dread a visit to the dentist. Encourage them to skip their opening night as Annie in the school play or the big history presentation they have been practicing if they seem at all uneasy. In fact, if your children show any signs of worry at all, step in and rescue them. Any loving parent would do the same.

It is natural to want to safeguard your children from all of the dangers that you perceive. However, if you are indulgent or overprotective, you are not helping your children develop the skills they need to become healthy, independent adults. When you restrict their freedom, they become more dependent. If you step in every time they struggle, your children will not learn to solve problems on their own, and they will not build self-confidence. And your children can not develop resilience if you never let them fail. Even if you struggle with anxiety, do not project your fears onto your children. They will learn to overestimate risk, and they will feel more vulnerable. As a parent, you can not eliminate uncertainty from your children's lives. It is your job to give them the ability to cope with a world that contains risk.

- How To Screw Up Your Children -

- Restrict your children's freedom.

(They will not learn to be autonomous.)

- Rescue your children every tie they are uncomfortable.

(Your children will not develop self-confidence or problem-solving skills.)

- Project your anxieties onto your children.

(Your children will learn to overestimate risk, and they will feel vulnerable.)

CHAPTER FOUR: SCREWING UP THE EVERYDAY

Ruin Your Children's Activities

If your school-age children are like most these days, their schedules are jam-packed with extracurricular activities. You are constantly shelling out money for the soccer club, gymnastics, violin lessons, art class, and anything else that will eventually make them a candidate for Harvard. In witnessing your children's triumphs, there is a high likelihood that you and your ex-wife will be at the same place at the same time, and there will be ample opportunity to infuriate her and, simultaneously, traumatize your children.

Your children's games, recitals, and performances are a great time to display your contempt for her in public. Make sure to sit on the opposite end of the school auditorium from your ex-wife or on the other side of the bleachers. Roll your eyes at her and call her names, you know how embarrassed she'll be. Once the activity is over, hold your position and force your children to decide which parent to approach first. If they chose their mother, give them the cold shoulder and threaten never to show up at their events again.

If you really want to taunt your ex, bring your younger, thinner, prettier new girlfriend along. It is the perfect place to show her off to the other parents in town, and a great way to boost your ego. You will feel like prom king again when all the soccer dads congratulate you on your score. (And did you mention she is just as hot in the sack?). The only people who will not be thrilled are your ex, who will be incredibly jealous, and your children, who will be mortified and embarrassed. But remember, you are dedicated to screwing up your children.

* * *

Divorce: The Art of Screwing Up Your Children

When you can not put your own feelings aside and build a cordial relationship with your ex-spouse, your children's activities will become a great source of stress and tension for them. They will be fearful that you will cause conflict at their soccer games, school plays, and music recitals. If you and your ex sit apart from each other at these events, you are making it even more difficult by forcing your children to choose which parent they greet first after the event is over. Having to take sides or show a preference will fill them with trepidation. They will then feel guilty for hurting the feelings of the parent they did not choose.

Your children's events should be their moments to shine. These are not the times to make a show of your new relationship. You are taking the focus of the event off of your children and making yourself the center of attention. Your children will also be embarrassed by your very public display.

- How To Screw Up Your Children -

- Sit far away from your ex at your children's activities.

(Your children will feel anxious having to choose which parent to approach after the activity has concluded.)

- Taunt your ex when you are in close proximity to your children.

(Your children will be embarrassed by your inappropriate behavior, and they will learn that it is acceptable to incite conflict.)

Preschoolers Need Cell Phones

Buy each of your children a cell phone, even if they are only in preschool. Teach your youngest children how to push just one button to call you anytime of the day or night. Let them know that when they are at their mother's house for the weekend, they can call you. Tell them to call you if they are unhappy, or their mommy isn't nice, or her boyfriend is scary. Let them know you will come right over to rescue them. Your children must know what a concerned parent you are and that you understand how scary it must be for them to be at their mother's house. Make sure they know that much like Superman, you will swoop in to save the day.

Teach your children how to use their phones to record their conversations with their mother or the conversation between their mother and her boyfriend. Having these recordings will give you helpful information to use against your ex-wife in the future. You are confident that your children will love to help you out. Download an app to their phones so they can digitally record their mother yelling at them. When you receive their audio- or video-recordings, be sure to reward your children with praise and gifts. Anytime your ex-wife has complaints about your parenting, remind her that you have recordings of her yelling at your kids.

Giving very young children a cell phone to call if they are afraid sets up the expectation that their other parent is scary, and there is something to fear. You will increase your children's anxiety level by suggesting that their time with their other parent is a time of danger.

Enlisting your kids in clandestinely recording their parent's conversations is wrong and harmful to your children. Your children will end up *feeling like they have betrayed their other parent. You are also teaching your children that it is okay to be sneaky and collect information on another person.*

- How To Screw Up Your Children -

- Buy your preschooler a cell phone.

(This empowers your children to call you whenever they are frustrated with their other parent rather than work out those feelings with that parent.)

- Suggest to your small children that they are afraid when they are at the home of their other parent.

(Your children will begin to think they are supposed to feel scared. Eventually, you may actually change their thinking, and they will express genuine fear.)

- Teach your children to use their phone to audio and video-record their other parent and show it to you.

(Your children will initially feel they are helping you out; however, as they grow up, they may feel guilty for betraying their other parent by spying on them.)

Administer The Silent Treatment

"You're dead to me." Proclaim it to your ex-spouse while wiping your hands together like you are brushing dirt from your palms.

Swear to yourself that from that day forward, you will never mention that woman again or even talk with her.

When you are in the same room, look right through your ex and act as if she does not exist, and walk past her without even acknowledging her presence. If she asks you a question, stay silent. If she tries to engage you in a discussion about your children, turn around and storm away. Do not hide this display of disdain from your children. Let them see your absolute disgust for their mother.

Make sure your children know that their mother is getting the silent treatment, and she will be ignored. You do not value anything she has to say, and you have no interest in hearing anything about her. Do not break your promise unless you are ordered to do so by the judge, or if you really need a favor from her.

CHAPTER FOUR: SCREWING UP THE EVERYDAY

Refusing to speak to your ex ruins your co-parenting relationship, making it impossible to discuss childcare issues and make decisions together for the best interest of your children. Your children must now struggle to get you both to agree on matters that concern them. This exposes them to increased levels of tension and conflict in private, and embarrasses them in public. Ignoring your ex also teaches your children that it is acceptable to use passive aggressive behavior to be disrespectful to others. They will model this behavior in future relationships.

- How To Screw Up Your Children -

- Ignore your ex-spouse.

(Your children will learn to be disrespectful to others.)

- Cut off the lines of communication for discussing parenting issues.

(This will hurt your co-parenting relationship, making joint decision-making very difficult, and exposing your children to more conflict and tension.)

Exploit Family Time

Healthy families eat dinner together most nights (at least that is what the experts say). You love this idea, because sharing mealtime gives you an opportunity to learn more about your children's play practice, homework, school friends, and, of course, what is going on at your ex's home. You can extract this valuable information from your children using the same interrogation techniques mentioned earlier in this book.

DIVORCE: THE ART OF SCREWING UP YOUR CHILDREN

You can repurpose any family activity into an occasion to screw up your children. Plan a game night, make a ritual of watching *Modern Family* with each other, go bowling every Sunday, and exploit these times together by using them to dig up intel about your ex.

If your children aren't very forthcoming, you'll have to employ another tactic: invite their friends along, and include them in the conversation. They have likely spent time with your children and your ex and will, unknowingly, reveal information. Kids do say the darndest things! And when asked, these little rumor mills will gladly spill the gossip on your children and your ex.

Scheduled family time is crucial, and you must insist your children cancel their plans and clear their calendars to be there. You wouldn't think of missing these important bonding opportunities under any circumstances, unless, of course, you have a date. If you have a chance to hit the town, all bets are off. In that situation, your children will just have to play videogames, eat dinner, and watch television on their own.

Chapter Four: Screwing up the Everyday

Using time during family meals or family activities as an opportunity to interrogate your children about your ex is a terrible idea. These special times are a chance to bond and get to know your children. If you upset your children by questioning them about your ex during these times, they start to dread mealtime and begin to look for any excuse they can find to avoid spending time together with the family.

When you draw your children's friends into these inquisitions, your children will revolt. They are embarrassed, humiliated, and annoyed that their friends are being dragged into their parents' conflict, and they feel powerless to stop you.

- How To Screw Up Your Children -

- Use dinnertime to grill your children about life with your ex.

(Your children will dread mealtime.)

- Have your children's friends over for meals so they can participate in the questioning.

(Your children will feel embarrassed and frustrated that you are using their friends to get information about them and their parent.)

Never Apologize

Do not apologize for anything under any circumstances. Never be sorry for anything that you did or that you did not do. This includes confrontations with your ex-spouse, your children, and perfect strangers on the street. To apologize is to admit you were wrong, and you are never wrong. You are perfect.

Just say that in a moment of complete vulnerability you realize you might not have been completely correct. Keep it to yourself. Do not admit it to your children, and NEVER admit any failure to your ex. Your modus operandi is to escalate the conflict and to win at all costs. (If you need a refresher, revisit the first few sections of this book.) Saying you are sorry would be a real tragedy. You risk diminishing conflict, reducing stress, and not screwing up your kids the best that you can. Furthermore, apologizing gives your ex something to use against you in the future. You do not want to hand your ex additional ammunition to use against you.

If someone has your back up against the wall and you must apologize for something, apologize to your children for the behaviors of their other parent. Be sorry for their father's demands, rules, idiocies, and incompetency. You feel terrible that he disciplines them when they get in trouble at school, and you are remorseful that your children have a father that can not cook to save his life. They really deserve better.

When you refuse to apologize, you are modeling irresponsible behavior. You are teaching your children it is not important to admit their errors or to seek forgiveness from those they have harmed. This type of behavior will severely affect all of their interpersonal relationships, and it will hamper your children's ability to have close friends and romantic partners throughout their lives.

Instead, swallow your pride, say, "I'm sorry," and set a good example for your children to follow. Apologizing is not showing weakness. It is showing self-awareness and humility.

- How To Screw Up Your Children -

- Never apologize to your ex-spouse.

(Your children will not learn to apologize to those they have harmed, and this will damage relationships throughout their lives.)

- Never apologize to your children (except for the failings of their other parent).

(Your disrespect for their other parent will be obvious.)

Get Creative

One final suggestion to help screw up your children: Use your personal experiences as inspiration for creativity. Create a fictional account of your divorce experience. Write a book, play, or short story about a crazy family in the midst of a horrible divorce. Include lots of details that are eerily similar to the circumstances of your divorce and co-parenting relationship, after all, truth is stranger than fiction. If writing isn't your thing, create an artistic expression of your divorce. Create a painting, watercolor, or even a sculpture depicting scenes from your marriage. You can tell yourself that your children will never notice these parallels (if you assume they will notice, you might hold back from including the really juicy stuff). If your children speculate that your fiction isn't so fictitious, deny, deny, deny. Publish your masterpiece, and spread your story far and wide.

You aren't fooling anybody, especially your children. They notice the similarities between your creative endeavor and their real-life experience, although it is disguised, and they know others will notice too. Your children will likely resent your depiction of their personal life, even if it wins a Tony, becomes a New York Times Bestseller, or ends up in a museum.

- How To Screw Up Your Children -

- Publish your writings about your personal experience of divorce. Thinly disguise the details.

(Your children will immediately recognize the characters and events in your work of fiction as mimicking their real-life story and will likely be angry with you for bringing attention to them.)

Final Thoughts: Getting Serious For A Moment

Afterward

If your goal is to screw up your children, getting divorced gives you a huge advantage, and following the advice in this book will ensure your success. Studies show that children of divorce are more likely to develop emotional and behavioral problems than their peers from intact families. These effects are responsible for poorer school performance on average and higher rates of physical illness, premarital sex, juvenile crime, incarceration, and drug and alcohol abuse. Children from divorced homes are also more likely to get divorced in the future, leaving their children (your grandchildren) at greater risk for these issues.

If you are a healthy parent, (and I assume that you are a healthy parent), you do not want to see your children suffer. There are steps you can take to reduce these risks, namely, avoid the bad parenting behaviors in this book at all costs, no matter how well-meaning or justified are your actions. If you recognized sections in this book that applied to you or your co-parenting relationship with your ex, and it made you uncomfortable, I hope the discomfort motivates you to do things differently in the future. Thankfully, children are resilient, and if you behave in a way that serves their best interests, you can minimize the potentially damaging effects commonly associated with divorce.

Final Thoughts: Getting Serious For A Moment

There are many important points in this book concerning your children's mental health, but some worthy of a final mention...

Unrelenting parental conflict is the greatest source of emotional pain for children of divorce and the number-one factor that impacts their wellbeing. It puts them in a no-win situation, smack in the middle of an ongoing fight between their parents. Children learn that yelling, demeaning, humiliating, and verbally abusing another person is an acceptable way to communicate, and they will revert to these behaviors in future relationships. Minimizing post-divorce conflict between you and your ex will be a huge relief for your children, and it is the most valuable thing that you can do to reduce their ongoing stress from your divorce.

Children need both parents to be active participants in their daily lives. Each parent may have strengths and weaknesses, but both offer unique and important contributions to their children's upbringing. When parents are not involved, or minimally involved, it serves as a great source of pain for children. They lose an integral part of their support system, and will likely conclude they are unimportant or unlovable since the people who should love them the most seem uninterested. This will result in low self-esteem and may cause depression and anxiety. Anything you do that impedes the relationship between your children and their other parent is harmful to their wellbeing. When you co-parent with patience, flexibility, respect, and forgiveness, you serve them best.

Children, not just children of divorce but all children, do better when their parents function as a team. Whenever possible try to present a united front, as it is comforting for children to know that the entity, "my parents," stands together for their best interests. It is best to present your advice as a mutual decision made by both parents: "Your mother and I agree you should..." or "Your father and I were talking, and we are concerned about..." It is important for your children to know that, although you two are divorced and apart as a couple, you will always remain their parents.

Parenting is, in many ways, a sacred task. However, it is not easy, and co-parenting after divorce is even more difficult. Bickering over childcare issues and making parenting decisions that serve only to upset your ex demean the important task of parenting. In the past, you and your ex have made mistakes, but in some instances, you have also managed to be agreeable, kind co-parents and make great decisions together concerning your children. Why make things harder than they need to be?

Regardless of whether or not you wanted the divorce, you have a responsibility to yourself and, most importantly, to your children to work out your issues with the divorce. Unresolved feelings, particularly anger and resentment, may compel you to behave in ways that ultimately harm your children. If you find you are practicing negative parenting behaviors, recommit to healing and strive to eliminate those behaviors.

If you are unable to change on your own, seek professional assistance. A psychotherapist can help you heal from your divorce and gain better control over your parenting behavior. A good co-parenting counselor will facilitate you and your ex discussing important parenting issues in a stable environment that effectively prevents the conversations from spiraling into blaming sessions. Co-parenting counselors will also present alternative ways of handling situations in a way that prove best for your children.

Your children love you and your ex, and you both play an important part in their psychological, physical, spiritual, and moral development. Give them the gift of healthy parenting, and commit to working together for their best interests.

I hope that you have enjoyed reading this book and seeing all the crazy things that parents do. But, I encourage you to avoid all of these scenarios and strive never to master the art of screwing up your children with your divorce.

About The Author

Howard Drutman, Ph.D., is a psychologist specializing in clinical psychology, and forensic psychology in family law cases. He regularly conducts child custody, parent fitness, drug and alcohol, and psychological evaluations and frequently testifies on issues related to the best interest of children in divorce cases. Dr. Drutman also provides psychotherapy, co-parenting counseling, parent coordination, and parenting plan development, and consultation with family law attorneys. His office is in Roswell, Georgia.

www.TheArtOfScrewingUp.com

www.AtlantaBehavioralConsultants.com

Made in the USA
Lexington, KY
30 January 2017